# SIR MICHAEL SADLER 1861-1943: ENGLAND'S INTERPRETER AND AMERICA'S ADMIRER

"Educate, educate, educate ..."

(*The Spectator* June 26$^{th}$, 1886 summing up the findings of the Royal Commission set up in 1885 to examine the causes of British depression in trade and industry.)

# SIR MICHAEL SADLER 1861-1943: ENGLAND'S INTERPRETER AND AMERICA'S ADMIRER

JACK SISLIAN

Nova Science Publishers, Inc.
*Huntington, New York*

**Senior Editors:** Susan Boriotti and Donna Dennis
**Coordinating Editor:** Tatiana Shohov
**Office Manager:** Annette Hellinger
**Graphics:** Wanda Serrano
**Editorial Production:** Jennifer Vogt, Matthew Kozlowski, Jonathan Rose, and Maya Columbus
**Circulation:** Ave Maria Gonzalez, Indah Becker and Vladimir Klestov
**Communications and Acquisitions:** Serge P. Shohov
**Marketing:** Cathy DeGregory

*Library of Congress Cataloging-in-Publication Data*
*Available upon request.*
ISBN 1-59033-409-4

Copyright © 2002 by Nova Science Publishers, Inc.
  400 Oser Ave, Suite 1600
  Hauppauge, New York 11788-3619
  Tele. 631-231-7269   Fax 631-231-8175
  e-mail: Novascience@earthlink.net
  Web Site: http://www.novapublishers.com

All rights reserved. No part of this book may be reproduced, stored in a retrieval system or transmitted in any form or by any means: electronic, electrostatic, magnetic, tape, mechanical photocopying, recording or otherwise without permission from the publishers.

The authors and publisher have taken care in preparation of this book, but make no expressed or implied warranty of any kind and assume no responsibility for any errors or omissions. No liability is assumed for incidental or consequential damages in connection with or arising out of information contained in this book.

This publication is designed to provide accurate and authoritative information with regard to the subject matter covered herein. It is sold with the clear understanding that the publisher is not engaged in rendering legal or any other professional services. If legal or any other expert assistance is required, the services of a competent person should be sought. FROM A DECLARATION OF PARTICIPANTS JOINTLY ADOPTED BY A COMMITTEE OF THE AMERICAN BAR ASSOCIATION AND A COMMITTEE OF PUBLISHERS.

*Printed in the United States of America*

"Surely what we in England really mean in our hearts by education is that great aggregate of the influences which come to us in our homes, at church or chapel, in daily life, in intercourse with our contemporaries, in love of home and father and mother – in all the thousand streams of influence and suggestion which in a free country converge upon each individual life, and shape ideals of conduct."

(Michael Sadler, "How far can we learn anything of practical value from the study of foreign systems of education?" Guildford, 1900).

"The Only Tragedy is Failure to Realize One's Capacity for Good."

(Michael Sadler, Master of University College, Oxford, and Elmer Ellsworth Brown, Chancellor of New York University, 1931, a jointly published brochure of their correspondence).

# CONTENTS

| | | |
|---|---|---|
| Author's Preface | | ix |
| Foreword | | xi |
| Chapter One: | Michael Sadler – Biographical, Thinker and Scholar | 1 |
| Chapter Two: | Sir Michael Sadler and the Third Reich | 9 |
| Chapter Three: | "The Crisis" - or the Second World War (from Sadler's diaries 1935-1939) | 27 |
| Chapter Four: | Comments as to the Authorship of a Secret Anonymous Memorandum-Document c. 1938 and the Memorandum Published in Full | 35 |
| Sadleriana-Bibliography | | 79 |
| Index | | 85 |

# AUTHOR'S PREFACE

This brief study of Sir Michael Sadler's work consists of four chapters and a Sadleriana-Bibliography: Biographical, Thinker and Scholar; Sir Michael Sadler and the Third Reich; The "Crisis" or the Second World War (from his diaries 1935-39); and Comments as to the authorship of a secret Memorandum Document c. 1938 – entitled, "Not to be Shewn to His Majesty's Enemies", printed here for the first time which has gone unnoticed in the histories of the Second World War. This Memorandum can be interpreted as a rationale indicating why and how a Second World War might be avoided.

(Full Title: *Memorandum* concerning the relationship of German incitement in *Czechoslovakia* to the international *Colonial Problem* and the public order of the world.)

"This document may be read and quoted from at the discretion of those to whom it is sent. But since publicity might destroy the detached enquiry essential to the author's method of approach it is asked that attention be drawn to his arguments rather than his name."

The writer makes out Sadler to be its author – arguments and reasons are substantiated.

The writer's main purpose in this book is to arouse interest on the reader's part in an extraordinary personality. Michael Sadler was a Comparative Educationist of the first order because his pioneering studies of educational systems went beyond what met the eye alone in national educational organisations. He wanted to know the impalpable forces that lay behind educational institutions in order to be fair to and discriminating in criticising or praising them. His countless works reflect this approach.

He thus laid bare the very close relationship between a people's politics and its national educational system. He doubted that a complete control and supervision of an entire national educational system could ever serve a true democracy, rendering the individual citizen subordinate to the rule of some State.

That applying such a principle to the world polity, that the individual person exists for the State and not the other way round, would end disastrously for the world's inhabitants, is the cryptic message of the Memorandum, which reflects Sadler's approach.

This publication would not have been written in vain if its readership begins to reflect on Sadler's summing up towards the end of his long life which somehow is irresistibly relevant to the ongoing debates regarding creed, schools and State supervision: "Is it towards an elaborately comprehensive system of all types of school, representing (so far as may be) every creed and many colours of conviction? Or is it towards some unified monopoly of education administered by the state and bound by it to presuppositions sanctioned by the State (and by the State) alone? In short (not to go further back) will it be to John Stuart Mill, or John Ruskin that the new model when it is completed, will trace its affiliation?" (See J.H. Higginson, ed. "Selections from Michael Sadler", Dejall & Meyorre, Liverpool, 1979 p. 192.)

J.S.

# FOREWORD

## By Dr. J. H. Higginson
formerly Warden of Sadler Hall in the University of Leeds

Michael Sadler, commenting on the writings of Matthew Arnold, wrote –

> "The harvest of a great man's thought ripens after his death. A writer often finds among his younger fellow countrymen an audience which enters into his meaning more fully than do men of his own age."

As I finished reading this assiduous study by Professor Jack Sislian, Sadler's comment floated into my mind. It is a felicitous perception applicable to this attempt to identify *"England's Interpreter and America's Admirer"*.

For many years since introducing Professor Sislian to the pioneering work of Michael Sadler in *Comparative Education* at a conference in the *University of Ghent*, I have watched his painstaking researches into the daunting quantity of Sadler's writings as indicated in the bibliography at the end of this volume.

Because of his particular knowledge of the German scene, Sislian is well-equipped to make his comparative analysis of

German and English society. How penetratingly he has done this can be judged by the reader. To this survey he links his account of Sadler's other lifelong interest, the diversity of society in the USA as a "melting pot" of nationalities.

Sislian's pre-occupation with "the secret memorandum" offers a challenge to historians. The skillful use of Sadler's wartime diary jottings brings vitality and immediacy to what might have lapsed into questionable hindsight. An attractive case is presented for the identification of the authorship with Sir Michael Sadler. Whether or not we accept this conclusion, Sislian has made available a most informative context of the Second World War, without sentimentalism or romanticism.

*Chapter One*

# MICHAEL SADLER – BIOGRAPHICAL, THINKER AND SCHOLAR

An exceptionally alert and reflecting mind as Michael Sadler's must have fully appreciated the privilege of having been born into a professional, radical and cultured family. His father was a medical doctor and a descendant of Michael Thomas Sadler (a pioneer of the Factory Acts), who travelled widely in Europe making profuse notes of the places he had visited. It is on record that Michael Sadler's father used to recite passages from Goethe's *Faust* as he rode in his carriage visiting his patients in the West Riding of Yorkshire. Thus, the parameters of his life and work coupled with his enquiring mind into problems of English national and international education, especially German and American, England's industrial rivals, were delineated.

Michael Ernest Sadler was born in 1861, in Barnsley in the West Riding of Yorkshire and was educated at a Preparatory School at Winchester, Rugby and Trinity College, Oxford. At Rugby he won a high scholarship and entered Trinity with a Classical Scholarship. He obtained a 'First' in Honour Mods., and a 'First' in Greats (at Oxford University an honours course or final examinations in classics and philosophy).

At Oxford, Sadler discovered his passion for History in its relationship to explaining and understanding the phenomena of education, first and foremost of England. This historical dimension stood Sadler in good stead throughout his long life as social and educational thinker when analysing educational problems in England, America, Europe and elsewhere.

In England, his abiding interest was in Adult Education which helped him become Secretary of the University Extension Lectures Sub-Committee at the young age of twenty-four, in 1885.

The American theory and practice of the 'melting pot' attracted Sadler's attention since it was an experiment in adult education. He left England for America in 1891/2, his first visit. His second and third visits were in 1902 and 1930, which was also his last. The lasting and profound influence these visits had on Sadler came to fruition when he became the first Director of the Office of Special Inquiries and Reports (1895-1903), London, which unquestionably was a direct emulation of the American National Bureau (now Office) of Education founded in 1867.

Among his numerous MSS in the Department of Western Manuscripts, Bodleian, Oxford, are many cuttings from American newspapers dealing with American efforts to teach English to and educate large numbers of Amerindians and immigrants to help themselves and their communities, which absorbed Sadler's attention.

Not only domestically were great American educational efforts made but also overseas – American colleges were built and maintained in Aintab, Aleppo and Istanbul; Beirut (c. 1861) and Cairo (c. 1920), each building an American University, while Africa and Asia were not ignored by American educational work, chiefly by American Missionaries.

Sadler traced the "spirit" of American educational effort to George Washington's Farewell Address: "Promote, as an object of primary importance, institutions for the general diffusion of knowledge. In proportion as the structure of a Government gives force to public opinion, it is essential that public opinion should be enlightened."

Industrially and production-wise and in business methods, as well, America and Germany had "forced England's hand." England was "backward" compared with American and German educational theory and practice having a bearing on production and trade. Yet, Sadler thought, neither America nor Germany could supersede the "Englishness" inherent in England's education. Writing in the "Contemporary Review" (September 1916) under the title "An English Education for England", he underlined, "The English view of education is distinct from the vision now prevailing in America and Germany. It is not merely a *via media* between two extremes, a middle way between State control of education on the one hand and the untrammelled unfolding of the individual's personality on the other. It is a distinct doctrine, or rather a practice in which a doctrine is latent."

Official America's total dedication to education and willingness to pay for the luxury of diffusion of knowledge at home and abroad among boys and girls, men and women, impressed Sadler deeply all his life. During his last visit to America in 1930, Sadler gave a comprehensive address to the Faculty and Students of Teachers College, Columbia University, stressing America's exemplary role in World Education, "But the United States, more than any other country has given drive and momentum to the new trend of educational thought and administration... ."

Sadler's preoccupation with University Extension work in England showed him that the success of his work lay in correcting work at the secondary education level. This view was also shared officially at higher levels in England which saw him become a member (the youngest) of the Bryce Commission on Secondary Education (1894-5).

On resigning his post in 1903 as Director he was appointed to a part-time professorship in the History and Administration of Education at the University of Manchester. In 1911 Leeds University invited him to become Vice-Chancellor, which he accepted. While still at Leeds he became President of the Commission on Calcutta University, 1917-19. On returning to England from Calcutta, where he had distinguished himself, he was created Knight Commander of the Star of India (K.C.S.I.), now defunct. On leaving Leeds University in 1923 he became Master of University College, Oxford, until his retirement in 1934. He died at Headington, near Oxford, in 1943.

Whatever his thoughts on education were, they were expressed within an historical framework. They could be of a damning nature, especially some of his thoughts on the misuse of State education for indoctrination of impressionable minds in racial or religious hatred. Yet such thoughts, although true to facts, never ended there. Sooner or later, Sadler would say, "Philip will be sober again!" Not unlike the French "encyclopédistes" there was, for him, an inexhaustible fund of optimism on which he constantly drew.

Sadler liked to contemplate on radical social changes, both in England and abroad, especially when they manifested forceful panoramic social and educational developments. The English Civil War and Oliver Cromwell's support of Dissent, which was still, according to Sadler, an unhealed wound, splitting the English nation in two down the middle; the two-mindedness of the English in educational provision and administration, should schools and what children are taught be a matter for State supervision and for State control, alone? England had opted for a mixed Aristotelian constitution, a true and balanced approach between private and public provision of school in society – Aristotle's *pan metron ariston*. What Society's greatest need in education was an education for judgement not obedience, knowledge or brilliance or eloquence.

Sadler's meticulous scholarship is evidenced beyond doubt by his monumental publications which clearly reflect his wide knowledge of educational organisation and administration in many countries as much as his reasoning powers and persuasiveness.

What he was mainly concerned with in all his addresses, lectures or writings was a "balanced" or "fair" approach when treating any educational subject.

In 1891, Sadler was full of enthusiasm if not adulation for what was happening in America concerning official or State support, materially. The American Trusts and Foundations were a boon to educational research. In comparison, the British government had been "backward" because it had entered at least a century late on the modern road of State interference and control of national education, in part through the absence of standardisation of popular education and partly because Britain's working people were less ductile than workers agglomerated in the large cities of the United States.

Some forty years later, c. after 1930, his last visit to America, Sadler's private thoughts somewhat modified his almost boundless praise for America, because in the meantime, common efforts in England were being made to recondition her education and her industrial methods, which were beginning to put an end to that "backwardness". Yet, he was not sure that governmental control was the right thing on the road to achieving popular education. But Americans understood English hesitations as they were more alive to the assimilative side of popular education through their familiarity with the phenomenon of 'the melting pot'.

Sadler was well aware of America's example to the whole world regarding giving everyone, everywhere, the chance to further his or her higher education through one's own effort. America had been the first to give scope on a magnificent scale to Americans to benefit from higher or university education. The world was following America's example, with varying degrees of delay or success, partly for psychological or economic reasons.

Sadler's legacy is that when all is said and done, any educational system is born in a social matrix, and national history and culture are the predeterminants of a national system of education, anywhere.

By way of summing up this chapter the writer feels nothing would be more appropriate than to reproduce below a short address Sadler gave to a school in England almost a century ago in which the educational aims of Germany, France and America are succinctly emphasised and compared. The reader might wish to reflect critically on them to underline for himself how much or how little has changed over the years concerning educational aims in the major countries mentioned above:

### ENGLISH AIMS IN EDUCATION

Speaking at the Whitcliffe Mount School, Cleckheaton, on Friday evening, the Vice-Chancellor of Leeds University, Mr. M.E. Sadler, said that, largely through the personality of the Headmaster, Mr. Joshua Holden, the school had become the centre of higher educational effort in Cleckheaton. He said that the educational system of each great country had its characteristic excellence and defects. America, for example, believed in opportunity and stimulated self-reliance, but was defective in quality of scholarship. Germany believed in educational discipline, excelled in scientific co-operation, but was too easily overcome by the prevailing intellectual fashion of the time. France almost worshipped the idea of equality, had preserved a fine artistic tradition in the things of the mind, but was still the victim of over-centralisation of ideas and too prone to prefer the safety of a petty official career to the risks of a more adventurous habit of life. England had a strong sense of the value of moral tradition; excelled in its standard of individual probity; but was intellectually amateurish, and timid in its handling of general ideas.

Summing up the chief characteristics of the English view of education, Mr. Sadler said that we believed in self-training and in struggling against difficulties, as tonic to character. But ill-directed forms of self-training did not cure pig-headedness. Secondly, we knew that education was a process which ought not to end with the close of the school or college career. Unfortunately, this insight into a fundamental educational truth had weakened our interest in problems of school organisation. Thirdly, England, though it believed in educational opportunity, had not properly organised it. Englishmen felt that it would be unjust, as well as unwise in the public interest, to exclude from high positions of trust those whose early education had been informal, unsuccessful or incomplete, provided that in their later development they had made up for previous shortcomings. But educational organisation, though necessary, brought with it the danger of regulations which would exclude from higher careers those who had failed to pass through conventionally prescribed courses of school preparation. Fourthly, Englishmen believed that the best things of education came through experience of life, through home training, through intimacy with contemporaries, and that, therefore, it was not simply or mainly a scholastic question. They saw that the great strength of an established system of education lay in its being part of a social tradition and that this, where good, should be conserved in the national life. This view, in itself just, had lessened our zeal for merely scholastic facilities and for improvements in the methods of teaching and of imparting ideas to the young. It had also encouraged group isolation in English training, because a strong tradition was generally found in a social group. Lastly, Englishmen at heart believed (though they were rather shy of admitting it) that education, if it was to get a grip on character, must have behind it the power of a great belief, whether in some form of religious faith or in an inspiring social ideal. But as we had inherited disjointed social ideals and were much divided in religious opinion, we had relapsed into a somewhat untidy conservatism and had been too ready to shirk the trouble and the risk of trying to think out our fundamental beliefs and a clear pattern of social relationships.

M.E.S. Nov. 21, 1913

*Chapter Two*

# SIR MICHAEL SADLER AND THE THIRD REICH

Sadler's first visit to Germany was in 1884, his last in 1930. In between he paid several visits as well. In 1884 he spent some time in Heidelberg learning German. His second visit was in 1895, just before becoming the Director of the Office of Special Inquiries and Reports, which took him to Eisenach, Ruhla, Jena, Leipzig, Halle, Cassel, Weimar and Dresden. His main concern during these visits was to inspect schools and to study experimental teaching. The stays although short gave him many new insights about current German ideas in education which only an eye-witness could get. At the beginning of 1897 he was in Berlin, left for England, and in September of that same year he returned to Germany, and spent some time in Hamburg. Sadler was very much impressed by Hamburg, a great seaport, especially by the progressive efficiency of German municipal administration and industrial development. But these impressions were also forebodings of future threats to England. In a letter to his wife in England Sadler wrote that transport of passengers in Hamburg was far better managed than in London and that the streets were cleaner, where even the old houses down by the docks were clean and well arranged. "The fact is," he wrote, "they are running right ahead of us." England was only at the beginning of the commercial struggle with Germany, for the Germans, after being idealists, were then flinging themselves into quite another line of life and rapidly excelling in it. The absence of commercial advertisements in Hamburg, unlike England, struck him most favourably. The only exception was "Mellin Nahrung". "His Nahrung (foodstuffs) are everywhere in red and green lamps at night." Mellin was a German by birth but the English had taught him this bad habit, which was taught in turn to the English by the Yankees. "It will spoil their towns too in time. Egoismus is beginning to rule the roost, and Beamtenthum (Civil Service) won't be able to control it forever ... I spent a good deal of time with the Erzeugnisse der Industrie (Industrial products) and extraordinarily interesting they are. Sheffield will have to look out. One exhibit delighted me – a packet of small explosive bombs to carry in your pocket when you cycle in order to throw these formidable things at dogs when they come barking at your feet." In 1912 Sadler paid visits to Düsseldorf, Wuppertal-Elberfeld and Barmen, Cologne, Mainz, Frankfurt, Mannheim, Munich, and Dresden. His last German itinerary, 1930, took him to Lübeck, Wismar, Schwerin, Stralsund, Greifswald, Swinemünde, Zoppot, Danzig, Marienburg, and Rostock and back to Harwich, via Denmark. Michael Sadleir[1], Sadler's son, who accompanied his father, reminisces, "Our last – and in some respects our most memorable. Hitler was a little more than two years and a half ahead; and although we had nothing beyond newspaper knowledge of the rise of National Socialism and certainly no prophetic sense that Hitler, as an individual, would prevail, we had more than a premonition that something was preparing in Germany and that the days of the Weimar Republic were numbered."

At one point during the journey home, his son tells us, Sadler remarked to him that he doubted whether he would ever go to Germany again: "Something is brewing and something I think we shall hate. This end of Germany doesn't want us English even now; before long those who will be in power will refuse us altogether, or make life so impossible that we shall stay away."

Sadler never went to Germany again, but in November 1934 Herr von Ribbentrop, the Reich's Foreign Minister, although officially holidaying in England, went to see him, as Hitler's confidential envoy with instructions to sound influential people on the question of mutual disarmament. Ribbentrop saw Sadler in the Master's Lodgings at Oxford and spent a weekend there. Sadler had invited guests to meet the German visitor. On Saturday, November 8$^{th}$, Ribbentrop, after dinner, sitting with others in a half-circle round the fire, had given a long and very skilful defense of National Socialism, saying that Germany, as a result, had been saved from Bolshevism, communist intrigues and Jews mainly of Polish origin. The Germans had become a "happy laughing people" after being disillusioned and demoralised under the Weimar Republic. His comments on post-Versailles behaviour of the victors were moderate and especially complimentary to Britain. His command of English was excellent.

The following day, Sunday, Ribbentrop had met Gilbert Murray and the Master of Balliol, conversations with whom he must have found to be frank and disconcerting. Sadler, after supper, had taken the offensive, "and for two hours made circles round the Nazi envoy", who with great effort kept his suavity under control. Sadleir mentions that Ribbentrop left on Monday morning leaving his father a note of thanks, written in a large sloping hand reminiscent of old Victorian ladies of a domineering character, which said that he was "still quite under the spell of old tradition, modern art and the most thoughtful and delightful of all hosts."

Five years after this meeting with Ribbentrop, Sadler entered the following in his diary for October $28^{th}$, 1939, on reading a speech by Ribbentrop in Danzig in that same year.

"Why did Ribbentrop come to me? Why did I entertain him? Because an old Univ. man, whom I had known long and who was a close friend of Ribbentrop, made a point of it; and, as head of this man's old College, I felt I could not refuse to be hospitable to him or Ribbentrop, who came together. Also because Ernst August, son of the Duke of Brunswick and grandson of Kaiser Wilhelm, was then an undergraduate at Univ. and in rather a special relation to me, and Ribbentrop wanted to see Ernst August.

Ribbentrop was a pleasant untroublesome guest. He was very keenly interested in our modern French pictures. With disparagement, I should say, that he acquired the manners of a super-wine Merchant – ingratiating but leaving an after-sense of arrière pensée. He spoke English very well – with slight American accent. (His commercial life – entirely creditable after his family losses in the war – had been in Canada). I did not think him particularly clever, nor very able. But he was persistent, a little inquisitive and (in retrospect) I remember that *irritation* or anger was not far below the surface, when he was told plainly what he didn't want to hear.

I did not want to have him as guest, because the persecution of the Jews had begun and I loathed the Hitler régime, and was afraid that Ribbentrop's presence as a guest might put me in an awkward position and involve courteous evasions. But it did not, because I decided that I must tell him what I believed.

On the last night of his visit he asked me whether, if Germany reoccupied, or threatened to reoccupy the Rhineland, I thought that GB. would resort to armed interference. After reflexion, I said I thought *not*. (The relations between GB. and France re the Versailles Treaty were not characterised at that time by full sympathy or mutual understanding.) I said that in my judgement we should regret Germany's unilateral action, probably protest, but not go to war.

But I added that a point might be reached at which unilateral breach by Germany of provisions of the Versailles Treaty would lead to war. I thought it right to warn him that this (in my belief) would be so – that, in short the elastic band would break."

About Adolf Hitler Sadler found that the first two hundred pages of *Mein Kampf* told the stirring story of a young man's courage in finding his way to a social ideal and flinching from no danger in his declaration and defense of it. Hitler had risked his life for the sake of a message, a mission. The belief in a way of life which involved a discipline of social relationships based on the supremacy of the State. To defend, publish and diffuse this way of living had become Germany's mission in the world. (Germans according to Sadler were mission-minded: Fichte had preached this, Wagner had made this the message of his music, a mission, which was metaphysical in some of its manifestations, militaristic in others)[2]. Hitler had smitten the Marxist idea of class war in its vitals, not because he himself defended outworn economic privilege, but because Marx had ignored idiosyncrasies of race. "One-sided, you say," wrote Sadler, "Yes, but so was Luther, and so is Karl Barth. Better be guided perhaps by Erasmus and Rheinhold Niebuhr. But many German minds respond more eagerly to the harsh emphasis of partisanship because they feel weakened by the subtlety of synthesis. Therefore the volcanic outburst, to which Hitler's propaganda has given vent, is of deep meaning to the world, not only to Western and Central Europe, but also to Russia, to Japan, to the Moslem peoples, and to the United States. It is a beacon of hope and of danger; it flares a message which may be a menace. The true answer to it will be found not in the enforcement of perilous "controls", not in repression, not in preventive war, but in the moral reconditioning of the economic life of those peoples to whom a much larger measure of individual freedom and of variety of opinion, than the German race feels itself to need, is indispensable to growth and effective action. We should set our economic house in order and resolve not to put up with artificial scarcity and half-strangled powers of purchase for consumption in a world now capable of producing unparalleled plenty. Intertwined with the spiritual factor in the mental tension of today are the economic factors. The non-German ideal of life should now assert for itself as great a freedom for self-expression as the German ideal is being given by the dramatic collapse of the German constitutional régime. ... The British answer to the Nazi Revolution should not be violence or diplomatic pressure, based on the ultimate sanction of force, but new economic experiment at home ... Things have got to a pass at which it is tempting, partly for reasons of policy, partly for good manners, to gloze over the bad side of what has happened in Germany. But if we appreciate the good side of the Nazi achievement, we are bound also, in justice to British convictions to declare our abhorrence of some of its methods and byproducts. In some of its manifestations, the Nazi Revolution denies equity and compassion. Some of its principles are subversive of liberty, as we know liberty: its practice is destructive of toleration, and if applied here, would be fatal to mutual confidence: some of its personnel (not Hitler himself or many of his colleagues) are no better than a camarilla which, having cowed its enemies, has seized the citadel of power. To submit to some of the Nazi doctrines would be, for us to deny the fundamentals of freedom. The more complete its apparent victory in Germany, the sterner our duty to protest against what is ruthless and reckless in its principles and practice."[3]

C.E. Carroll, editor of the Anglo-German Review,[4] a Review which was intended to foster greater understanding on the English side for Germany's Nazi Revolution, sent Sadler the First Number with a letter dated November 23rd, 1936 requesting him to subscribe to it as he knew Sadler was interested in German affairs. Sadler subscribed for the following five numbers, enclosing cheque. "Your request," wrote Sadler to the editor, "touches a point upon which I feel so deeply that I must ask you to be so good as to allow me to write plainly as grave principles of national policy are involved. My whole life has been coloured by what I have learnt in Germany and from German philosophy, literature and education. I have had for nearly 50 years intimate friends in Germany and can never fully express my gratitude to them for their affection and guidance. They have not been all of one way of thinking. On the contrary, I feel deep regard for some still living who have left the country of their birth. Many years ago I wrote what England owes to German thought and practice in education, and at what points the two countries differ on fundamental points of administration and principle – e.g. Allgemeine Bildung, in particular, and State Control of all education, in general. But in spite of these fundamental disagreements, England owes to Germany a debt which we shall never forget.

And there are aspects of German educational reform, since Herr Hitler became Führer, which I rejoice in as far as this general tendency is to abate the undivided sovereignty of intellectual attainments and to lessen the forces which have produced in many countries a false distinction between the so-called "educated classes" and the otherwise educated people. But to my grief the present régime in Germany is challenging to a degree which I regard as fatal to freedom and to self-respect, the right to express individual opinions on questions of human duty, purpose and allegiance. I deplore the sneaking and feel that its prevalence in Germany poisons the atmosphere and can only lead to violent and deplorable reaction.

For these reasons I cannot do anything which – while expressing my profound attachment to German people and to the culture and geniality of German life – might be taken as signifying indifference to what I believe to be pernicious in the pressure now exerted in Germany upon opinions and beliefs which are regarded with disfavour by the auxiliaries of the present régime."

In England, on the other hand, there was freedom of thought and of utterance and she belonged to a small group of countries where opinion was still relatively free. But history showed that this had not always been so. There was nothing in the English character which made the English indisposed *at times* to curtail liberty of utterance.[5] "Will such a time recur? East and West of us in Europe lie countries where controls have been set upon this or that kind of intellectual freedom. And when we cast our eyes over present-day Germany and make the fullest allowance for the zeal and ardour of hundreds of thousands of young people in the Nazi ranks, it is difficult to avoid the suspicion that, along with much that is sane and purposeful, there are symptoms of neurotic transport."

Speaking at the James Seth Memorial Lecture on the State and Education, 1936, University of Edinburgh, Sadler pointed out that fundamental questions of individual liberty and of freedom of conscience are raised by the action of those Governments which were determined to control and colour opinion by the political use of all the agencies of intellectual and social education. Never before had so many methods of indoctrination lain ready to the hand of the supreme authority in the State. By regimentation of teaching in schools and Universities, by strict control of broadcasting and the use of wireless propaganda, by limiting freedom of public discussion and even of conversation by telephone, by censorship of books and by regulation of the press, a resolute Government bent upon silencing and eliminating opposition, could (for a time at any rate) establish a mental tyranny and crush critical resistance to its policy and principles … It had to be admitted that all education implied some degree of indoctrination. But the assumption that, by the exercise of strict control of education in all its forms any government could give permanently whatever character it pleased to the community under its sovereign control, and that it was possible to devise disciplines and infections which would determine the thoughts and convictions of all men and women, was still unproved. To question this underlying assumption, however, was not to deny the value of energetic State action in securing educational change. "We may think that Herr Hitler's ideal of racial purity is mistaken. We may feel horror at the indignities, impoverishment and exile which under his leadership have been inflicted in Germany upon those of non-Aryan stock or of communist opinion. But we can appreciate the good side of many of his educational ideas, and especially his efforts to secure a healthy physique in the young generation, his wish to bring divided social classes into close comradeship during their impressionable years, and the stress he lays upon the moral value of hard manual labour in tasks of public improvement." The brightest hopes of the future, however, did not lie in the Totalitarian State but in a combination of State authority with the intellectual and spiritual freedom of individuals and groups within the community.[6]

All his life Sadler had worked to see Britain do her utmost to equalise social opportunity and that in educational matters she should as little as possible restrict individual initiative. The road of adventure should be kept open to minds which develop late. As a result of Germany's practice of stereotyping conditions of entrance to professions and to professional training, latecomers with exceptional gifts but with defective preliminary qualifications had been excluded. As an example of this practice Sadler, referring to *Mein Kampf* says that Adolf Hitler was shut out from the School of Architecture in Vienna, because admission depended on attendance at the Building School, and admission to the Building School required a full certificate from a Middle School which, through the death of his father and mother, Hitler had not been able to stay long enough at the school to get and so the fulfillment of his artist dream had no longer been possible.[7]

Reflecting on the basic difference between the English and German structures and approach to their respective educational systems, Sadler observed:

"The crucial difference between the history of German education and that of English during the nineteenth century lay in the different use which the two countries made of the power of the State. In Germany that power was exercised unflinchingly, with great forethought and clearness of purpose and without any serious resistance from public opinion. In England it was used reluctantly, with deliberate rejection of any comprehensive plan of national reorganisation and in the teeth of opposition which had to be conciliated at every turn. Germany adopted without serious misgiving the principle that national education is a function of the State; England hesitated between two opposing theories, the theory of private (or of group) initiative and the theory of State control. Germany worked on system; England, on compromise. England attempted an accommodation between two conflicting principles; Germany committed herself to a consistent theory of State control and acted in accordance with it. As a result, Germany has constructed an educational system which works with fairly simple machinery; England has a complicated machinery, but no well-defined system of national education."[8]

It was on the basis of this assessment that Sadler judged the English educational system to be "nearer the truth" compared with Germany's, or expressed differently, the ideal educational system would have to reflect "variety set in a framework of national organisation". In practice, for example, this would mean there would be several roads leading to the same examination. (In the Federal Republic of Germany there are today some ten different ways a student seeking admission to a University or Hochschule can qualify for.)[9]

Sadler maintained that intellectual and moral advancement of the human race called for the free play of criticism and it was this freedom to criticise, to differ and to experiment that the Third Reich was then curtailing or suppressing. When he talked to friends from Germany, Italy and Russia he was struck by the fact that with some exceptions the young people were admiring and energetic supporters of the new regimes. What attracted them most in Nazi-ism, Fascism and Soviet Communism was the hard bodily work and training imposed on them, the physical labour, plain living and beflagged demonstrations which they were required to undertake, practice and attend. A new and stringent claim was made on them in the name of the State and the community and they rose to it. The silly stuff they swallowed from Rosenberg and Banse and other myrmidons, not to speak of the lunatic part of the high-spirited book *Mein Kampf* and the orations of Goebbels, Göring and Dr. Rusk, the Minister of Education, might make them drunk but sooner or later "Philip would be sober".

It was this new emphasis laid on bodily fitness for public service that Sadler thought would appeal some time to young English men and women, or boys and girls. English youth could not stand even a well organised Nazi demonstration without getting bored or seeing the funny side of it. But barring the foolish trappings and with good sense talked between-while, Sadler thought a programme not unlike Hitler's educational plan might not be distasteful to the young English mind. Sadler pointed out that the bodily side of the new regimes in Central Europe was the result of a passionate new kind of nationalism which wanted to wipe out blots of defeat and memories of political ineffectiveness as well as usher in a new ideal of liberal education. The first had got entangled with much silly and pretentious and mock-scientific theorising: the second had shown itself first in the very country, Germany, which had suffered most from too intellectualised form of liberal education for the élite of the nation. What was gradually coming, Sadler believed, was the dawn of liberal education for everybody, not for the élite only or for the privileged classes alone but for all. And of this the new state of mind among the young was a presage.

For these reasons he did not think it unlikely that in England a government would impose on the English for a time by orders in Council rules of uniformity in many crucial matters of political and economic opinion in the national interest and for the defense of the realm. Sadler felt that it might be worthwhile for England and her inhabitants to be obliged for a time to submit to rigorous control of conduct and opinion, but only if that control was accompanied by a strenuous and scientific and uncheeseparing effort on the part of the government to provide for all of England and for the younger generation especially new, abundant and generously equipped opportunities for the training and exercise of the body to grace, skill, self-control and public service. Such a transfiguration of England's educational ideals would be worth the price, Sadler thought, of some years of intellectual repression and the cutting of the claws of criticism. He admitted, however, that the English were intractable under that kind of State tutelage.

In the young English generation then growing up, Sadler did not see any marked enthusiasm to go to prison or to meet the firing squad at dawn on behalf of John Stuart Mill's refined and equitable ideal of toleration and party-coloured liberty. The great majority of young English men and girls seemed to him to be more interested in games, travel, swimming, human affection and hairdressing than in Sir Stafford Cripps or Sir Oswald Mosley. Sadler did not think it likely that England would have an English Hitler or an English Stalin or an English Mussolini. But some of the good ideas which Hitler stood for, and some of the good ideas which Stalin represented and some of the tonic which Mussolini had administered to Italy, would seep into British administration and policy.

But it would be naïve to imagine, Sadler warned his contemporaries, that there would be a swift awakening among English schoolmasters and dons to the coming change in the focus of a liberal education. It had taken a long time for English schoolmasters at the late Renaissance to notice that young Shakespeare and his contemporaries had liked the pedagogue Holofernes well enough as a man but had not thought much of his curriculum. It had taken a long time, after the decay of the medieval trivium and quadrivium for Oxford dons of that time to realize that the old Gothic floor had gone rotten under their feet. The very virtues of English education, and they were superlative, stood in the way of early acceptance of or even perception of the need for revolutionary change in educational perspective, methods and values. The walls of Jericho had been fragile compared with the walls of the Local Examination Delegacy in Merton Street. And by making the discipline and exercise of the body the centre of all liberal education England did not mean the adoption of those systems of physical training which were like ghosts of militarism standing around graves in a civil cemetery.

The writer hopes to have at least partly succeeded in depicting to the reader one or two insights into the working of Sadler's mind when looking comparatively at the German and English educational scenes, which put an end to many outworn social and economic orders and ushered in new ones. With prophetic vision Sadler already saw in the early 'thirties that the modern world had entered upon an era of accelerated revolutionary change, because of the swifter transmission of thoughts and of news, and the quicker passage of people and of goods from one land to another. Because one fundamental part of the problem which mankind was endeavouring to solve was economic, all parts of the earth were in some degree involved in the revolutionary inflammation taking place in Germany, Italy and Russia just to mention the European continent. But because the unrest in English minds was spiritual as well as economic the course of the revolution would proceed at a different pace in different regions, since in some countries there had been a fuller preparation than in others for the perception of new claims upon individual duty and human obligation.

Sadler would have us share his persuasion that the economic life of mankind is interpenetrated by a power which was not economic but a spiritual force which came from a region far beyond the scene of our bread-winning. This educational philosophy had very wide implications of a grave nature to all involved in the work of education, which according to Sadler, was very far from being an affair of schools and colleges alone or of the Board of Education or County and County Borough Committees or Church Assembly or teachers' societies. It always involved a multitude of other agencies which had their roots in the history of a nation, and could not be transplanted in another nation. It was against this sociologically analytical background that Sadler passed judgements on the Third Reich.

## ENDNOTES

[1] Michael Sadleir, Sir Michael Sadler's son, novelist, biographer and art collector, author of "Fanny by Gaslight", first published by Constable & Co. 1940, was a member of the publisher's Board. This section draws initially on his book, "Michael Ernest Sadler: Memoir by his Son," London, Constable, 1949.

[2] *Examples* "Göring addressed an impassioned appeal to the entire German nation to collaborate with him in his new task of supervising the four-year plan of self-sufficiency in raw materials. He disclosed nothing fresh about the plan but he said much about the reasons for it, the sacrifices expected and the reward in the shape of a mighty independent Germany, secure without and secure within, which would be enabled to fulfil the mission in the world which they all believed was hers. ... His speech relied largely for effect on the picture of a hostile, callous, uncomprehending and chaotic world hemming in an ill-used, orderly, hard-working Germany." (A sinister speech by Göring in Berlin, *Times*, October 28th, 1936.) "We will, of course, take up the fight against the world for our colonies." (Goebbels. Berlin, *Times*, October 30th, 1936 in article entitled "Threat to Colonies".)

[3] The New Germany and Peace. Review of three books by Sadler: *The Intelligent Man's Way to Prevent War*, (Ed.) Leonard Woolf. *Why Nazi?* Anon. and *Nazi Germany Explained*, Vernon Bartlett. Macmillan.

[4] The offices of the "Anglo-German Review" were at 6, Warwick Court, W.C.1. In order to win over British sympathy one could read in that number "Human nature that has striven towards the light for centuries does not go bad under years of adversity" in an article "Britons who served Germany" by Lt.-Col. B.G. Basker, DSO., FRGS., F.Hist.S. Another example: "Dr. Frank, Reichsminister of Justice, in his goodwill speech to 25 legal men from the UK said that the visit of members of the English legal profession was particularly welcome and

appropriate at a time when Germany was engaged in reorganising its legal system and trying to remodel it, in part at any rate, on the system in force in England, the country which had always been looked on by German lawyers as the home of Justice."

[5] Sadler: *"The Outlook"*, Oxford Magazine, October 26$^{th}$, 1933 where he also mentions: Roger Williams, to whom religious liberty owes much, had to fly from England to Massachusetts and from Massachusetts in turn to Rhode Island. John Robinson, pastor of the Pilgrim Fathers, had to fly from Norwich to Amsterdam and Leyden. The Jesuits, to whom we owe much in the defense and readjustment of the Catholic tradition, were driven from England to Douai. John Locke had to fly for intellectual shelter from England to Holland. And little more than a century and a half ago Joseph Priestley had to escape from Birmingham and London to Pennsylvania. In a lecture Sadler delivered at the Wives' Fellowship at Oxford on October 7$^{th}$, 1934 he said the following on a similar subject: "England, even England, was not always like this. Less than two miles from this room, the University of Oxford passed in Convocation on July 21$^{St}$, 1683 a "judgement and decree against certain pernicious books and damnable doctrines destructive to the sacred persons of Princes, this State and government and of all human society. This judgement and decree, rendered into English were published by command at the Sheldonian Theatre in the same year. A number of books by Hobbes, Milton, Richard Baxter, Julian the Apostate Dean Owen, Fifth Monarchy Men, George Buchanan and John Knox, as well as the Solemn League and Covenant, some Roman Catholic writings and Quaker doctrine about the Inner Light in its bearing on politics were "deemed, judged and declared" by Convocation of the University of Oxford to be "false, fallacious and impious", and most of them also heretical and blasphemous. All members of the University were interdicted from reading them. And Convocation ordered that "the before recited books be publicly burnt by the hand of our Marshal in the court of our Schools". Hitler does this kind of thing, but of course such demonstrations are foreign to the English disposition and temperament of today." Sadler thought that the

Germans ought not to have put up for that long with the Third Reich. They ought to have fought it instead. He asked himself if, were he living in Germany, he himself would have succumbed to the Hitler régime and after reflecting over it he thought he would have, just like so many Germans had (MS Bodleian, Oxford).

[6] This paragraph is based on Sadler's Lecture on "State and Education, Robert Owen, John Stuart Mill and Adolf Hitler", which he delivered on May 12$^{th}$, 1936, University of Edinburgh. MS.

[7] Based on Sadler's Lecture on "Democracy and an Elite", which he gave at Leeds Luncheon Club, February 12$^{th}$, 1934. MS.

[8] History of Education", c.1910, by Sadler.

[9] Apart from the Gymnasium the Abitur can be obtained at the Abendgymnasium, Sozialakademien, Fachhochschulen, Kollegen, Kollegartige Institute, through the Sonderprüfung, Nichtschüler Reifeprüfung and Begabtenprüfung.

*Chapter Three*

# "THE CRISIS" - OR THE SECOND WORLD WAR -

(Source: Sadler's diaries 1935-39,
Department of Western Manuscripts,
Bodleian Library, Oxford.)

Sadler termed the Second World War and the events leading up to it as the "crisis".

The disappointment he felt in events on the eve of that war was as bitter as profound. He had once before in his prime as a man of just over fifty gone through the holocaust of the First World War and knew from past experience the calamitous effects of war. As a man of almost eighty at the outbreak of the Second World War he went through much suffering of emotional strain caused by mental anguish, as the many distressed jottings and entries in his diaries testify.

The thought of yet another war to live through, this time a far more formidable and merciless one, and one which he thought was wholly unnecessary, for he dismissed economics as a *casus belli* to start a war between Germany and England, must have caused him at times intolerable agony.

In this connection Sadler's mental bearing is reflected in an entry in his diary some four years before the beginning of hostilities in 1939. "Have an *Ahnung* (a premonition) that Germany may make a sudden attack on South Russia (Ukraine) for the extension of territory. Via Poland, semi-neutral; Italy, preoccupied with Abyssinia and Franco-Russian Pact not yet signed." The detection of some inconsistency in Sadler by an outside observer might be based on Sadler's looking coolly at the probable development of events and at the same time refusing to believe in the ultimate development of a clash of arms between Germany and England and other nations. This did have a debilitating influence on his thinking rationally which, to the present writer, is further proof of Sadler's acute mental pain, which often led him to turn his back on sordid reality and indulge in wishful thinking, that things certainly would be acceptable in the end, without the necessity of the world's having to go through a major war for a second time. He never gave up hope right up to the last moment that war somehow would and could be averted. When this did not happen it is not too much to say, that it shook his belief in the common run of Germans. Yet he was not harsh in his judgement of a people from whom he had learnt a great deal and to whom he remained indebted as ever.

Speaking to the "Boys of the City of Oxford High School" in 1936 Sadler told them that a government, if armed with far-reaching powers and not resisted by open opposition, could exert stringent control over the expressed opinions of teacher and taught. It could curtail variety of formulated judgement. It could browbeat belief and by propaganda colour the contents of the mind. By penalties, harsh mercy or compulsion and it could remodel a school-system and heartless, it could punish minorities, whether racial or political, at its pleasure.

"The Crisis" - or the Second World War 29

Continuing the talk Sadler mentioned the questions that were occupying his mind then.

"As a result of recent happenings several questions now occupy our thoughts. Will the ultimate results of this repression of freedom and of this reorientation of schools be salutary or permanent? Will the price paid by the community through harsh treatment and through subjection to espionage and dictation be commensurate with the advantage which may be gained by lessening of class distinctions in schools and by the closer adjustments of the supply of highly educated young people to the effective demand for their services in professional or administrative careers? And which elements in the educational changes which have been instituted by the Fascist, Nazi or Soviet governments are specifically political or partisan, and which are evolutionary and ameliorative?"

Sadler learnt later on where repression of freedom had led to in Germany: violence and cruelty, expulsions of the native population from large areas of its secular homelands, the banishing of hundreds of thousands of men and women to the interior of Germany as forced labour, mass executions and deportations to concentration camps, the plundering of public and private property, the extermination of the intellectual class and manifestations of cultural life, the spoliation of the treasures of science and art and the persecution of all religious belief. These were unparalleled in all human history.

His entries in his diary for the years 1938 and 1939 especially reflect the turbulent times and his reactions to them.

Commenting on Adolf Hitler's speech at the *Nazi-Parteitag* in September 1938 Sadler writes that the tragedy was that most of the English felt affinity with German *Gemütlichkeit* (cosy, warm and friendly) and found it hard to adjust their minds to the state of semi lunacy to which propaganda and gangster rule had reduced the German people.

"We realize that Hitler and his advisers defy the rule of law and discard compassion and that a stop must be put to them some time. But they are so strong that they cannot be stopped without a conflict which say, for decades, will ruin Europe." The worst one could say of British policy during the month, was that it had been equivocal. That came from the "two-mindedness" of the English and Sadler concedes that as a result of this "many misunderstandings on the part of foreign observers, friendly or hostile" might be the price.

If the English could not stand up to the gangsters then, there would be worse trouble later on and they would have fewer friends. According to him the war was a war of ideals. If the English went to war what should they be fighting for, he asked himself. Because of the genuineness and comprehensiveness the answer is given as he entered it in his own hand in his diary:

> "I have tried to get this clear and can't. 1. Standing by France if she is endangered. Sound, and we have promised. 2. Prevention of threats to British economic interests in the Danubian area and Near East. I can't judge the magnitude of this issue but feel that no British economic interests should be allowed to bring on a world war. Apart from its being (in the long run) bad business, I would give up British prosperity rather than invoke such a "preventive" war. 3. To go to war because of Czechoslovakia is a distressing question. 4. Defeat of the Nazi-Regime violence, cruelty, anti-Semitism, vast ambitions and denial of the laws of nations. Against the German people we have no anger. We are astonished at their acquiescence in Nazi domination. But we regard them as under the spell of admiration for Hitler and fear of his myrmidons. Hitler, Himmler, Goering, Goebbels and thousands of others are enemies of what we believe to be the true interests of the human race."

Allowing that much of the social policy of the Nazis had good points he envisaged that the war would be a Crusade against the Nazi-Gang and its doctrines. Was a world war the best way of dealing with that evil and could not the English try a Crusade of Propaganda?

And in the same entry in his diary, he writes,

> "In Church early this morning, I felt a strong assurance that there would not be a world war at present. A curious, impressive mental experience. One felt that the movement of the mind came from a level below articulate analysis – as if one were sensitive to something that is *part* (underlined by Sadler) of reasoning and of observation but prior to any conscious assembling of pros and cons."

On Czechoslovakia's losing the *Sudetendeutschland* Sadler remarks, "What, if done earlier, would have been disinterested guidance, becomes when done by us under duress a dirty trick." While Munich was imminent he wrote on September 25$^{th}$, 1938, and evidence pointed to war,

> "But deep down and below the level of discursive reason, I feel that there will not be war – at least a war in which we took part – whether for good farseeing reasons or for plausible I can't explain, or justify this feeling, but record it."

And one day before Chamberlain, Hitler, Mussolini and Daladier reached an agreement on September 30$^{th}$, 1938 Sadler still refused to believe that war was inevitable. "A day of grave issues. But I still feel *au fond*, that war will be avoided, tho' all the outer signs are the other way."

Sadler was among the Eighteen Prominent British Citizens who signed the "Manifesto on Peace and Cooperation" on

January 27th, 1939. This Manifesto was among his diaries and reads,

"A spirit of uneasiness broods over the world. Men and women in every country are uncertain what the next weeks and months may bring.

They see huge armaments piling up on every side. They see plans being made for civilian defense and they realize only too vividly that war under modern conditions between highly organised States can bring no good, but only death and destruction to countless homes irrespective of age or sex.

They see our civilisation, to which men and women of all classes and in all countries have contributed, threatened with the greatest catastrophe in human history.

It is time, if we are not to be too late, that men of good will who value the fruits of civilisation, who have no hatred or spirit of revenge in their hearts and who desire in all sincerity to live on terms of friendship with their fellow men in every country, should speak across the frontiers to those who feel as they do in order that they may use together their gifts of heart and mind to co-operate in preventing the supreme catastrophe and in breaking down the artificial barriers of hatred by which we are in danger of being divided.

We in Britain have no desire to dictate to others. While resolutely determined to maintain our own liberty, we stand for peace – a peace of equality for all and of justice for all. We stand for the rule of law in the relations between States – the only basis on which our civilisation can be preserved.

We recognise that no civilisation if it is to survive can be static, but no nation will find a lasting solution of its problems save in a spirit of cooperation with others.

We appeal above all to the leaders and people in the Great German Reich at this moment of power and influence in their history. We appeal to them to use those great gifts by which they have for centuries enriched our common heritage in all fields of human knowledge and activity and to join with us in a supreme effort to lay the spectre of war and enmity between nations and, in the spirit of free and willing cooperation by which alone can their needs and ours be satisfied, to build with us a better future so that we may not only preserve civilisation but hand it down to our children enhanced by our experience."

It was Lord Halifax who had requested Sadler whether he could add his name to the list, the others being The Marquess of Willingdon, The Earl of Derby, Viscount Dawson of Penn, Lord Norden, Lord Macmillan, Lord Stamp, Montagu Norman, H.A.L. Fisher, G.M. Trevelyan, Lord Eustace Percy, Dr. Ralph Vaughan Williams, Sir William Bragg, Sir Arthur Eddington, Sir Edwin Lutyens, Sir Kenneth Clark, John Masefield and Lord Burghley.

This Manifesto was given to the Press and BBC on January 27th, 1939 and was also distributed in Germany to all cultural institutions.

Sadler, knowing the German scene well did not overestimate the effect the Manifesto might have. Kenneth Clark viz. on receiving a letter from Sadler and the Manifesto signed by him, wrote to him saying that he agreed with Sadler that the Manifesto would not have any great effect on the German people as a whole but that according to the Foreign Office information there was a considerable body of rational men and women in Germany especially in the learned professions, science, medicine etc., who would be glad of some such expression of their views.

Soon after the Second World War broke out Sadler noted the following reflection in his diary which delineates his personality as a man of thought ever preoccupied with understanding the history of man and his world in order to read some sense into human phenomena and development brought about as result of the interaction of the world of men and things. Towards the end of 1939 when there was a good deal of soul-searching being done in England about her War Aims, he reflected,

> "With increasing clearness, I feel that, whatever may be the issue of this War, the world (not Europe only) has entered upon an era of conflicts. In the $15^{th}$ and $16^{th}$ Centuries the root cause of major wars was the Discovery of the New World. In the $17^{th}$ century the root cause of the Thirty Years' War was the realisation (scientific experiment and Descartes) of Man's Place in Nature, which led to a conflict between discrepant ideologies in government and belief. In the $19^{th}$ Century, Economic Revolution and its bearing on Human Society was the prime cause of the swift acceleration of wealth and commercial enterprise leading to political ambitions, of the self-defensive religion of Nationalism (Fichte and List), of the heady phantasies of Imperialism (Kipling, Fr. Naumann, Mussolini) and of the War of 1914-18, of the war between Japan and China, and of the Spanish War 1937-8. But now what lies before us is the Disclosure in the Nature of Man of unfathomed depths of devotion, cruelty, endurance, malignancy, stoicism, charity, self-will, belief and mischief. War, as J.L. Garvis says, is now (because of aeroplanes) in three Dimensions. But it is also a Fourth Dimension – the psychological. And in this Fourth Dimension there is still a profound mystery."

As a result of the annexation of Sudetendeutschland by Germany Britain had become a part of Europe by obligation and contract and "Baldwin went as far as he dared when he said our frontier was on the Rhine. Our frontier now will be in Czecho-Slovakia – the new Czheco," was how Sadler summed up England's entry into Europe in 1938. By a twist of fate in history, it might be said, that it is still so at the time of writing (A.D. 2002), and especially so after England's joining the European Common Market on January $1^{st}$, 1973.

*Chapter Four*

# COMMENTS AS TO THE AUTHORSHIP OF A SECRET ANONYMOUS MEMORANDUM – DOCUMENT C. 1938 AND THE MEMORANDUM PUBLISHED IN FULL

While carrying out initial research work on Sadler in Christ Church College, Canterbury, at Leeds University and the Bodleian Library, Oxford, and handling Sadler's innumerable MSS the present researcher unearthed the following secret anonymous document at Canterbury, given to Dr. J.H. Higginson by his son, Michael Sadleir, after Michael Sadler's death. The title of this highly confidential Memorandum already suggests why its author wished to remain obscure. After studying this document for several years the present writer has come to the conclusion that the Memorandum was written by Sir Michael Sadler, unless in fact it is proved that someone else is the author. So far the present researcher's efforts to trace the author of the document have failed consistently. Apart from the then British Museum he has tried the Foreign Office, London, as well as the House of Commons Library through its Deputy

Librarian and the Public Records Office. (These attempts were made through the present writer's personal connections, through private channels, such as friends of persons working in these documentation centres in London and through persons known to the writer who have especially access to these places, for example journalists working for leading papers in Great Britain. All to no avail, unfortunately.)

The above-mentioned conclusion was reached after comparing very closely, for over three decades now, Sadler's countless MSS having relevance to the content of thought, tenor, and linguistic style of this Memorandum. As far as the writer as well as the greatest living authority on Sadler, Dr. James Harry Higginson of Canterbury are concerned, no one has taken a scholarly interest heretofore to help to identify the document's author. The writer wishes to submit Sadler's name, as the most likely person to have written the Memorandum, for the following reasons, explanations, and reflections, mentioned below.

Before doing this, however, a few words must be said regarding the significance of finding this document to the body of scholarship in the world.

The irrefutable importance of this Memorandum especially to German historians lies in the fact that according to the present author this is the first time that the existence of this document is being disclosed to readers anywhere. To historians of the Third Reich this document must be new. Nowhere has the present researcher come across any reference to it in the many authoritative histories for the period 1933 to 1945 or since, whether the authors of these reference books were German or British. For the first time since it was written, obviously immediately before the outbreak of the Second World War, this historic document is now being made available to scholars of History and Political Thought. The main significance of the

Memorandum is found in the views and reasoning expressed therein, which it would be safe to say, were shared by a small group of very influential British personalities. That such efforts were being made in England in order at least to postpone the outbreak of hostilities if not to avoid the Second World War completely is proved by this Memorandum. That these efforts were being made by loyal British personalities rather than British people sympathising with the Third Reich must certainly be new to German historians of the period. Inevitably the gist of the arguments resorted to in the document reflected the British view of how to preserve British interests for ultimate imperial survival despite England's being prepared, according to the reasoning in the Memorandum, for concessions to Germany in the fields of politics and economics with a view to her exercising greater influence in the world polity which, it is argued in the document, were definitely her due. These concessions to German interests would, in Sadler's views, which he already had expressed at the beginning of the First World War, eventually lead Modern Germany to "A free Germany (which) is a necessary asset for the world's civilisation, and a dominant British interest." (Sadler's Diary (his unwavering belief since 1914), August $12^{th}$, 1914, p.15.)

**REASONS, EXPLANATIONS, AND REFLECTIONS:**

1. The lucidity of the language (Sadler's inimitable English usage and literary style) and the conciliatory tone of the style betray Sadler's sympathetic understanding of Germany as a great power and people, a recurring theme in many of his writings on modern history of Germany or

Prussia. (E.g. Sadler, "Modern Germany and the Modern World", Macmillan, London 1914.)

2. This conciliatory tone, but firm in its contours, expresses Sadler's lifelong conviction that England and Germany had much to learn from each other because both countries' *Weltanschauung* (world view) drew its inspiration from the same source of life and duty. The educational or social systems, as well, of Great Britain and Germany sprang from and were governed by closely related ideas of life and duty. (SADLER, "History of Education Collection of Lectures", Manchester, c. 1910.) Within this framework of Sadler's thought the reasoning in the body of the document that Germany's concern to protect her Empire was "legitimate" is understandable (GOEBBELS: "And we shall certainly take up the struggle for our colonies." Speech in Berlin, 1936, obviously referring to Germany's lost colonies at the end of the First World War. In 1936 Germany had no colonies.)

3. That war between the English and the Germans was unthinkable because misery, deprivation, and sacrifice were too high a price to pay for by two highly civilised nations for settling their differences. Sadler repeatedly mentions this in his Diary as the outbreak of the Second World War gets nearer in time. (SADLER, Diary, 1939. Bodleian Library, where his 13 large Cardboard Boxes of MSS were made a gift of by his grandson Richard Sadler in the late sixties. Today, they are housed at the Bodleian Department of Western Manuscripts, Oxford.)

4. The argument, that peaceful accommodation of each other's international political and economic aspirations could be attained. It is hardly conceivable to the writer that any other Englishman but Sadler in an official capacity could have proposed at least such a partial

proposal, for fear of being accused of betraying British interests. Sadler's stature in national life was such that he would have never been accused of coming to terms with Germany which was aspiring to play an important role in world politics and of which she was convinced that it was her right to claim. Sadler could allow himself such reflections not only because of his most intimate knowledge of Modern Germany for over fifty years but because a man like Herr Joachim von Ribbentrop, German Foreign Minister during the Third Reich, as Adolf Hitler's secret emissary was sent to him to sound British reaction to changes taking place in Germany.

5. Understanding of German grievances because of her having reached the level of a Great World Power but with "delay" compared with English. This is a recurring subject with Sadler in dealing with the development of English and German politics and social life in their relation to British and German educational systems. But the greatest protagonist of this theory of "late comer" to the imperial scene in the world was Professor Seeley, Oxford. (As empire builders "we (the English) were there first"), whom the present researcher wishes to compare with Professor Heinrich von Treitschke, an extreme German nationalist, a contemporary of Seeley's in the nineteenth century. Treitschke wanted a German Empire through war against the British Empire, and dislodge the latter. Sadler's reaction to the German threat was, "The British have had longer experience of a great position in the world." (SADLER. Paper – MS c. 1915.)

6. To the last Sadler did his very best to draw the attention of his countrymen and that of the Germans to the folly of waging a war once more against one another. Sadler was

one of the Eighteen Prominent British Citizens who signed the "Manifesto on Peace and Cooperation" on January 27$^{th}$, 1939 and on that day it was given to the Press and BBC and was also distributed in Germany to all cultural institutions.

7. The psychology of the Germans is depicted in the Memorandum as "restive", to which Sadler in his earlier writings also refers to as "the Germans are a nervous people". (SADLER on "Modern Germany and the Modern World", Macmillan & Co., London, 1914.)

8. The general spirit of the document is fully in line with Sadler's personality as gleaned from his writings, thoughts, and long and profound reflections on and relations with Germans and Germany for over half a century, a lifetime for any man of his intellect, knowledge and sensitivity.

9. The document betrays its author to be a man possessing intimate knowledge of the German "national character" and commanding a broad-based approach to the subject he is handling. Both these qualities were reflected by Sadler when treating problems of national life, aspirations and education in England and Germany comparatively and are attributable almost entirely to him as the most likely person to have written the Memorandum. As an example the following ought to be mentioned: "In order to understand the policy and achievements of a nation, we must study (so far as a foreigner may) its ways of thinking and the inner failings, as well as the virtues, of its character. We should be on our guard ... when we try to analyse the mental habits and the moral characteristics of the Germans. They, like ourselves, are manifold in origin and in social tradition. They, like all modern peoples, have

a complex psychology." (See SADLER on "Modern Germany and the Modern World", *op. cit..*)

10. "Some peoples are congenitally fear-ridden by heritage of their ancestral memory." This thought is expressed as thirteenth argument in the attached Memorandum and is also found in Sadler's own MSS, verbatim.

The above-mentioned reasons, explanations, and reflections give the writer sufficient cause for his conviction that the Memorandum's author can be no other than Sadler. If ultimately facts prove that the document was actually written by him, a mental association based on evidence might support further the present researcher's conviction that it was Sadler who wrote the secret Memorandum. From the very beginning of his career Sadler looked upon his Office of Special Inquiries and Reports, whose first Director he was, 1895 – 1903, as the Intelligence Branch of the Board of Education in London. (See especially "PAPERS relating to the Resignation of the Director of Special Inquiries and Reports, May 18th, 1903, Board of Education", Presented to both Houses of Parliament by Command of His Majesty, HMSO Cd. 1602.) Furthermore, without attaching undue importance to the following, it is nevertheless of some significance, since Sadler's choice of words do suggest, that he would have liked to go to Germany incognito: "What would one not give in these early months of the fourth year of the (First World) war, for the power to go to Germany and, with full knowledge of the language or without one's identity being known or questioned, to talk freely with men and women of all ranks and opinions?" (Sadler's introduction to FRIEDEL's book "The German School as a War Nursery", London 1918).

Part of the title which is explicit about who is allowed to read the Memorandum – "Not to be shewn to His Majesty's Enemies" – suggests that the document is the result of Intelligence Activities, which in turn gives the present writer ample reason to believe that the Memorandum's author is Sadler, if it will be remembered that he considered his work as "Intelligence" and he himself as the educational "Intelligence Officer" serving King and Country then as a loyal Civil Servant. Sadler's original letter as drafted by him proposed the title of the incumbent of the Office as "Director of Educational Intelligence" although the then Vice-President of the Committee of Council on Education (Mr. Acland) had suggested "Director of Special Inquiries and Reports" and the Secretary to the Board of Education (Mr. Kekewich) wrote to the Vice-President says that Military Intelligence was well understood but he feared the use of "Educational Intelligence" might subject the Board of Education to a certain amount of criticism. (See "RESIGNATION PAPERS", *supra* pp. 3-5.)

A copy of the original Memorandum in full length is attached to enable the reader to make up his own mind concerning its author.

## NOT TO BE SHEWN TO HIS MAJESTY'S ENEMIES

*MEMORANDUM concerning the relationship of German incitement in CZECHOSLOVAKIA to the international COLONIAL PROBLEM and the public order of the world.*

*This document may be read and quoted from at the discretion of those to whom it is sent. But since publicity might destroy the detached enquiry essential to the author's method of approach it is asked that attention be drawn to his arguments rather than his name.*

MEMORANDUM concerning the relationship of German incitement in Czechoslovakia to the international colonial problem and the public order of the world.

1. Before the relation of the international colonial problem to war in Europe, and to German incitement in Czechoslovakia, can be demonstrated, some premise of control must be chosen, upon which effective observation can be made in relation to the world. These broad definitions seem the most practical.
2. In its simplest form a colony is a land or subject race controlled or influenced by an alien or guardian state, other than that which would be the sovereign authority, where there is no alien or guardian state controlling or influencing a subject race or a group of peoples upon that land. Within the definition comes lands and subject races such as are to be found in the Crown Colonies of the British Empire, and in mandated territories under sanction of the League of Nations. But colonies include lands which are backward productively, and incompletely

politically evolved states, citizens of which are unlike subject races when judged by outward manifestations of their forms of government, but who either tacitly or openly are under the sovereign influence of one power or of some powers, for one purpose or another.

3. Threatening problems of international colonial unrest are not concerned with present colonies only, but also with the forces of conflict that throughout the world surround potential colonies.

4. Potential colonies are lands which are backward productively, and peoples which are backward politically, when judged by the best standards of energy and the best ideas of the times. The backward are backward irrespective of whether or not stronger powers are in a strategic position to occupy their territories and govern them. Backward lands and races are included in this definition when it is not easy to cite sovereignty of an alien power, or powers amongst whom sovereignty is in dispute. Thus, all lands may be considered as potential colonies wherein an alien state may contribute, dispensably or indispensably, by political or military control, by permeation of its peoples, or by indirect influential authority towards apparent progress or obvious exhaustion of its peoples. A definition so broad seems confusing and unhelpful. Nevertheless in classical times definitions of colonial activities suited to practical minds of statesmen came nearer to the one above than to current restricted definitions.

5. The international colonial problem is complicated by what ensues indirectly from the high strategy of the most important powers owning colonies and not owning colonies. Military hegemony is obvious and is resented openly. But naval hegemony is not obvious and is resented

by ill-feeling that is not defined clearly. The Monroe Doctrine (which guards the integrity of South American states) and the allied military power of Great Britain and France (which protects the integrity of many small states in Europe, Asia and Africa) prevent the expansion of Germany in Africa, South America, and through Eastern Europe to Asia, and impede the expansion of Italy and Japan.

They seem good to the democratic allies, but bad to the powers who do not share in the benefits of them. The Monroe Doctrine is destructive to the welfare of the citizens of the state whose integrity it protects. Exclusively wielded naval and military power provokes resentment from enterprising citizens of Germany, Italy and Japan, who are obstructed from promoting the well-being of subject races in militarily protected but ill-governed lands. Citizens of states without colonies feel deprived of the liberty implicit in the right of the other states to colonial expansion. They resent being excluded from the enjoyment of benefits obtained from organising inferior peoples, and they arm themselves to establish this right.

5. The activities and desires which have to do with the capture and possession of colonies are often described in various ways according to demands of rhetoric, when the object is to persuade persons of justice or injustice calling for special statement. These activities and desires may be classified briefly under the following headings which have to do with activities and desires of men who colonise. Consideration of them is therefore related to the welfare of the world rather than to welfare of any particular empire or state. Some of them have appeared variously disguised

in a correspondence about German colonial ambitions in the Times:-

1. desire of men of powerful mind and character to spread the benefits of a superior civilisation.
2. zeal of religious men to spread good ways of living.
3. desire of ambitious men to expand the domination of their authority.
4. desire of an enterprising commercial class to create new wealth in foreign lands by organisation of cheap labour, by buying and re-selling new products, and by starting new industries under protection of commercial systems which by upbringing they have learned to trust.
5. desire of a manufacturing commercial class to acquire secure and substantial new markets for their exports.
6. anxiety of men of highly trained middle classes for new opportunities of new service which, must be satisfied by keener and more ruthless competition at home when not satisfied abroad.
7. desire of industrialists to acquire access to minerals and raw materials in order that they may not fear victimization in competition with industrialists in states now possessing exclusive access.
8. anxiety concerning pressure from poverty and over-population.
9. concern to establish sound currency and credit broadly based upon the enterprise and wisdom of a unified political group.
10. pressure of over-educated classes for opportunities of easier service.
11. desire for the adventurous to explore new land.
12. wanderlust.

The above are desires and anxieties of individual men concerning activities associated with colonisation. Conflict concerning the fulfillment of them drives men to organise as states for war. The individual desires are spiritual, civilised, ambitious, religious, commercial and adventurous and they are expressive of apprehension of internal pressure. Considered as they are felt by men who seek to fulfil them they are not terror striking nor inspired by aggrandisement, nor wreaking in horror and revenge. Men, whether they be British, French, German or Japanese, will not cease to be urged by noble desires towards inferior peoples while there are still inferior peoples. Citizens of some states, deprived of such rights, will not cease to resent the rights of others. The problem agitating Europe now is to make war impossible in so far it is related to resentment of colonisation.

6. The following are urges of states and are the outcomes of desires of various groups of citizens who compel their states to organise in order to provide them with outlets for colonisation.

   13. citizens urge statesmen to organise the state in order to obtain outlets for their energies in dominions abroad.
   14. citizens urge statesmen to organise in order to obtain expansion for commercial activities.
   15. citizens urge their statesmen to organise and perfect military instruments for the purposes above.
   16. industrialists urge statesmen to organise to acquire raw materials for military purposes.
   17. citizens, angered and ashamed by absence of prestige, urge their statesmen to organise in order to obtain prestige.

As expressed by citizens of states now organised to keep their colonies, these desires seem God-fearing and salutary. As expressed by pent-up citizens of states not permitted to colonise they seem macabre and threatening. War is inevitable so long as citizens of states with colonies resent citizens of states without colonies organising in order to obtain colonies. War therefore is caused by mutual resentment of interference with rights. War is most likely to occur when refusal to define or allow rights precludes thought or discussion concerning them.

7. Together these activities and desires are expressive of the urges of states, classes and individual men. They belong alike to citizens and classes of states with colonies and of states with colonies. As possessed by citizens of states with colonies they seem virtuous and are more definite as activities than as desires, and as possessed by citizens of states without colonies, they seem criminal and are less definite working from the minds of citizens in twisted self-expression and verbal statements that sometimes are unpardonably incoherent and undistinguished. Because of their complex and paradoxical nature they are not regarded definitely as rights by state, a class, or an individual citizen. Only when observed in relation to the world and the spirit of man can they be deemed as rights and can judgements be made concerning them. To regard relations of activities and desires to rights in this simple way, is the only known method of avoiding war by statesmanship. It is the point at which judgement of virtue and crime must be tempered by wisdom and mercy wherein statesmanship becomes essential.

8. A desire that has no outlet in activity is a property of the mind alone. No man knows what desire he possesses until his desire becomes an activity. The simplest and most

direct quality of desire is urgency. A desire, therefore, need not be either searching or definite, it is likely to be misrepresented in statements made about it either by its possessor or by its opponent, and it possesses no character as a right until opposition to its urgency makes of it the concern of a more general polity. If a desire is urgent enough it will be interpreted and respected as a right. The seventeen named desires are all urgent to citizens of certain states who are dispossessed of their rights to activities in relation to them by the accepted polity of the world. Preference between them is impossible so long as they remain as desires in the minds of disorganised citizens. Choice for the German citizens, German classes, and the German state is not as simple as the fatal choice that in the myth confronted Paris. To the imagination of a potential lover, desire to possess many ladies is not so definite a form of absorption of the mind as activities towards the possession of one lady. Moreover none of the seventeen ladies named is suited by herself to be a mate, nor is she likely to prove trustworthy while her attentions may be distracted by advances from more reputable suitors, or more glamorous rivals. Hobbes wrote:

> "But the most frequent reason why men desire to hurt each other, arises hence, that many men at the same time have an appetite for the same thing which yet, very often, they can neither enjoy in common, nor yet divide it, whence it follows that the strongest must have it, and who is the strongest must be decided by sword."

Hobbes is vague concerning the meaning that can be attached to "the same thing". Men possess appetites not only for "things" that are the same, such as land, money, raw materials which modern schoolmen declare to be valued dearest by citizens. Desires lead citizens into a complexity of energetic movement, so devious and paradoxical that all that men, classes or states, do or aspire to, cannot be named conveniently nor specified. Rights to activity which men decide by sword, before they learn how to decide them by justice and honour, cannot be distinguished in terms of money, land, dominion, sex, etc.. They are associated with the passionate aspirations or individual beings, classes and states. Aspirations when thwarted become possessed by envy, jealously, hatred and resentment. Thus concerning any urgent desire that is thwarted there is always the imminent and inevitable danger that the thwarted possessor of the desire may be unmanned. Activities and thwarted desires associated with empires are not as they appear in popular statements of colonial policies and ambitions. Passionate aspirations in regard to empire seem least acceptable to citizens of the democracies in the awkward and ugly fashion in which sometimes they are expressed by pent-up citizens of frustrated states.

But the disregarding behaviour that evokes this hideous awkwardness is a constant menace to the manliness of citizens in states without colonies. The allies resent the interference of new states in the policy of the world as if the new states were upstart speculators without the manner to mix among gentry. The contempt with which their rights are disregarded and their grievances ignored breeds hatred and revenge. The organisation of German citizens in order that they may crystallise desires as rights to activity belongs not only to their determination but to their fear of disorganisation in their urgency. To expect constant nobility of vivid expression from pent-up citizens in degrading turmoil of bitter frustration is pitiless and ignoble. Urges to activities while they remain in the mind as desires are felt by the citizens of states without colonies as hateful deprivations. They are not comprehended clearly as seventeen separate deprivations, but suspected vividly as cause of injury, and excuse for revenge.

9. Citizens compel their statesmen to organise for war in proportion to their urgency to crystallise their desires into rights as activities. When a state prepares for war, citizens while engaged in unsatisfactory activities of peace, try to establish recognition of rights to new activities by organising for war. War, to citizens of the world who suffer acute pains of deprivation and dispossession is a vague and forthright method of establishing several rights to crystallise several desires into several activities at once, it is not an end in itself. To citizens possessing rights satisfying their desires to be active in relation to colonisation and empire, peace is a method of enjoying rights to activities established as outcomes of war. Full activity in peace therefore is not the opposite of war, it is a product of the outcomes of wars. War is resented by those who thrive upon the products of past wars as a threat by their enemies to interfere with their exclusive rights to activity. Therefore, peace can be enjoyed without fear of interruption only when rights to activity that theretofore have been gained or kept during war are adjusted during peace.

10. If the above diagnosis of the grievances of citizens of certain states without empire or colonies is true, it is clear that to allow Sudeten German lands to belong to Germany is not likely to lead to a settlement of long-term German

grievances. The outcome of this policy may be the immediate release of tension for a short time. It may postpone thought, discussion, and judgement upon German rights and grievances. It may lead Germany, together with new allies that may rally to her, to seek further expansion by more affronts to the public order of the world. Thus, there may follow increased apprehension of military domination by Germany. Likelihood of eventual world war may seem more inevitable. Faced by these likelihoods the allied democracies must now consider whether Germany's further expansion eastward is a more inconvenient and mischievous price than the world desires to pay in order to compel Italian subservience to the allies by Italian embarrassment in Austria, whether the public order of the world will remain in the keeping of the allies if the allied citizens consent to further expansion of concentrated blocks of German citizens to Eastern and Central Europe.

11. The democratic empires are vulnerable, as never heretofore, from the immediate action of organised hostile states wherein the citizens seek to disturb present rights to activity established by citizens of democratic states as outcomes of past wars, for the monopoly of their empires. Concentrated in the democratic capital cities workmen who control and guide pivotal forces. By their knowledge and service they maintain prosperity and empire for themselves with minimum loss to individual freedom. The mode of modern living attracts the best working citizen of all types into vast, densely inhabited areas of offices, and dwellings. Depleted in man-power, shattered in nerves by the long war of 1914-1918, obsessed by enjoyment of present responsibilities, the allied citizens are obstinate concerning their rights, and sluggish in their attitude

towards new war. The military responsibility, the administration, the credit and the trust organisations of the British Empire are dependent upon guidance emanating from decisions taken from day to day in London, and from the momentum of traditional service kept vigorous by the fact of thriving prosperity in London. In the same way, France is dependent upon Paris. But neither Germany nor Italy are dependent upon leadership concentrated in one great city. Germany and Italy are depleted in man-power and shattered in nerves. But they are obsessed by the urgent desire to increase their responsibilities, and eager to enter upon new war with this aim. Their military responsibility, administration, credit and trust organisations, emanate from decisions taken in order to establish the rights of German citizens in relation to the world and the momentum of this new service is kept vigorous by an organisation concentrated upon this end. The aggressive military organisation of totalitarian states is a constant menace to allied sovereignty. At the outbreak of war there is nowhere in England or in France whereto the directing minds and the daily business of work carried on in London or Paris could be transferred within the few seconds of absolute safety. It seems likely that important buildings of the democratic capital cities in Europe will be destroyed. Public servants and workers will be killed, wounded and suffocated, thrown into panic, absorbed in demoralising concern and pity for women and children. Two or three generations of indispensable persons will be slaughtered together. Civilised activities and order throughout the democratic empires and the world will be dislocated by disorderliness arising from lack of guidance and impotency of control. Within the dictatorship cities there will be less disturbance of the momentum of their wealth and power. In comparison with advantages the German citizens hope to gain Germany will suffer little damage as an immediate outcome of success by terrorising German enemies. Therefore, the powers possessing colonies today are vulnerable in an acute, terrible and menacing way by the air power and aggressive organisation of citizens of states seeking to interfere with their rights.

It is wiser to exaggerate dangers than to ignore them carelessly. War now is waged by soldiers and policemen against civil populations and civilians. Its outcomes are the exhaustion, persecution and death of countless worthy citizens, the destruction of treasures, buildings, and businesses. The jubilant triumph of either set of participants is a trivial matter. It is not in the interest of the general polity of the world that a monstrous great war should be brought on mistakenly, or that its approach should be resisted indeterminedly. If another European war is fought in the present condition of military organisation and armaments, memory of western civilisation after this way may be as nothing compared with the misery and desolation of the defeated, and the madness and the remorse of the victors. A short-sighted and careless view ignoring the inclination of pent-up men towards romantic and evil domination when exposed to the contempt and irony of their enemies, is based upon foolhardiness rather than upon wisdom and courage.

12. It was exposed by French statesmen to Queen Elisabeth of England that she should marry the King of France because France and England could have governed in combination the known world at that time (so it was believed by French statesmen). This debated alliance never came

about. British and Scottish statesmen began to realize that England and Scotland, since they were then invulnerable from Europe, should combine as two states of one realm. Thus:

> "This sea-kissed isle, the storms, and wind, and mist
> Now beat upon in constant watchfulness,
> Hath grown a kingdom, whence the earth around
> Go men for love of honour and keen life,
> To build an empire that shall rival hoards resist
> By power dovetailed in joints of truthfulness,
> A wondrous citadel, whose unseen mound
> Stands firmly grounded on stern rocks of strife."

The citizens of the British Isles, undisrupted by local envies and jealousies, combined to begin an empire, isolated from feuds of the princes of the disunited Europe. Less than four hundred years later, the continent of Europe and all subject races relying upon its guidance and control are exposed to many ill-effects of internecine war and menace. Yet the peoples of Western Europe are invulnerable from the rest of the world if they refrain from war among themselves. Even supposing the Maginot Line invincible, England and France, if they stand together and exclude Germany from the democratic alliance, cannot govern the world with certainty and assurance. Britain and France therefore must contemplate either an offer of friendship to Germany and her allies, or the annihilation of Germany and the dispersal of Germans. Perhaps German grievances may be redressed with magnanimity and with fewer and worthier risks in regard to the establishment of world polity than are attached to the prospect of European war. The last war was entered upon in innocent wonderment, as if the undesired passage of it would be incidental to the times. It continued four bloody years. Therefore new wars will be entered upon responsibly, as a means of changing the status of peoples, or criminally, as undesirably outcomes of collisions of the forces of neglect and frustration. Earl Baldwin has declared that the British frontier is today on the Rhine. But similar grave reasons of high policy, as once urged the uniting of England with Scotland, and later urged the alliance between Britain and France with a joint frontier on the Rhine, (as proposed to Queen Elisabeth) – but an alliance between the British Empire and the Great States of Europe including Germany. The rough implications of these new and changing strategic factors are to be found in the awkward reticence of democratic statesmen, and the perplexed aimlessness of high policy.

13. Some peoples are congenitally fear-ridden by heritage of their ancestral memory. Each generation is cowardly in that it is born too obstinate to permit colonisation, and too stupid to assimilate superior civilisation. The grim trail of barbarian conquest and persecution in the mountains and valleys of central Europe has left behind in the sensitive memories of the mixed occupants of these lands resentment of humiliation and indelible traces of defeat. The stability of government in Central, Eastern and Balkan Europe is upset by the animosities of inferior peoples claiming unmerited attention. Peoples and territories which British statesmen regard as the quicksands of Central and Eastern Europe may seem to their inhabitants like bulwarks of independence but to German citizens who intend to colonise them they are backwashes of civilisation. These backward peoples are likely to remain unfitted for colonial enterprise, except upon the supposition of everlasting German military

hegemony. Clandestine encouragement of German expansion among them cannot be divorced from its consequences to the changing polity of the world, now in keeping with the allies. Germans apprehend a menace of dispersal and disintegration as an outcome of German defeat in another European war. It is unlikely that they do not apprehend the same type of menace as an outcome of German attempts to absorb Central and Eastern Europe. Thus it comes about that German citizens believe Germany to be encircled – by the domination of the allies if they try to expand seawards and to the West and by the danger and futility of enterprise in the Balkans if they try to expand eastward.

14. The allied misapprehension that Germany seeks to dominate Europe by military force is based upon a misreading of German character and history and upon misinterpretation of present events. It ignores the speed and restricted responsibility of German unification in the nineteenth century. It neglects that the type of imaginary power which dominates as might for the sake of might, is as like or unlike power in recent German history as it is like or unlike power in recent allied history. Even the military prowess of Prussia is neither harsh nor exceptional, it has been accompanied by conscientious regard for honest enquiry and zeal for social reform.

Where political authority is dependent upon military power, the dependence is a product of ignorance of the responsibilities of power. It is a problem to discover where this ignorance lies, whether it is in relation to the polity of the world or in relation to the internal polity of Germany, it is the allied statesmen who ignore worldly responsibilities, whether it is German statesmen who ignore either responsibilities in regard to the evolution of the German state, or worldly responsibilities in relation to the claims of their citizens to recognition of worldly rights, and so on. Once internal power is acquired and safeguarded against interference by external rivals, confidence in dependence upon trust becomes a better means of government than military oppression. To mistake the methods of the German state in acquiring power in relation to allied animosity for means of German government, when once Germany has acquired power, is a convenient misinterpretation of German character. It misleads the allies in to refusing concessions to German friendliness. To continue in obstinate refusals to consider and discuss friendly concessions on the likelihood that this propaganda is honest is bad policy. The organisation of Germany into an exclusive formidable totalitarian state threatening allied domination is a novelty. But in relation to world polity and the responsibilities of world sovereignty it is no more shocking than the evolution of trade unionism in the early nineteenth century. When those who support it consider that its claims to rights have been considered justly it will cease to be menacing. Germans refuse to live as outlaws in the polity of the world. For them life is worthless without prospect of expansion, either across the sea or in Europe. As a state Germany is organised to establish the rights of her citizens to activities, and to fight for the freedom of Germany in relation to a rich and abundant world. German citizens risk massacre and dispersal, preferring to work for fulfillment of their rights to activities, as if Jews in gallant conflict with the enmity of the Roman Empire.

15. The European situation in relation to Germany is dangerous. The problem of world polity in relation to

Germany is difficult. Panic has arisen, because in the minds of citizens and of statesmen also perhaps, the difficulties of world polity are confused with sensational dangers that threaten Europe. Statesmen and citizens are obsessed by the desire to minimise exposure to dangers that terrorise imagination. They are confounded into regarding the ending of these dangers as their paramount duty. Being obsessed by them they neglect striving towards solution of difficulties of world polity and sovereignty. War is an outcome of the mortal incapacity of statesmen in relation to world polity. On occasions unreality can seem grimmer than reality. Trembling obsession with physical excitement of exposure to utterly disregarding menace is morbid panic. The impressive wizardry of menace when juxtaposed by its silly complement, specious urgency to avert spiritual debasement, conjures an alluring sidetrack compelling the most virtuous men into an abyss of destruction. The citizens of a state may be educated in a way that it is in conflict with ugly dangers the evil nature of which they have been taught to trample upon as tempting, and to ignore as corrupting. The aggregate momentum of their activities may drive them unwittingly towards a fatal act of historic significance, such as the suicide of Cato. Herr Hitler and his advisers are persuaded that they perceive this tendency to decadence in the British people, they mock it without being certain whether they can force their British rivals to self-destruction, or compel their British friends to share destiny with their brother citizens of Germany.

16. New orders of polity come about either by bloody revolution or because they are interpreted and put into

force by statesmen alert to dangers arising from resentment or injustice. Menace of war in Europe, as related to present world polity, is equivalent to a threat of revolution. Sudeten German irritations and grievances in Czechoslovakia were in danger of being overlooked when not underlined and exaggerated by German propaganda. Herr Hitler has elected to champion them for reasons other than a particular concern for Sudeten grievances. Inconveniences, embarrassments and excitements enable Herr Hitler to draw attention to the urgent need of Germany to create and assure opportunities for worldly enterprise of German citizens. They advertise the extent to which German leaders are urged by all classes to increase military armaments. They invite the allies to realize that in the minds of German citizens the close organisation of the modern German state is fitted more adequately to obtain redress for urgent German grievances in relation to the world than a liberal or democratic organisation of the German peoples, such as would be preferred by the Allies. Herr Hitler believes that the outcome of the grim menaces of German military organisation may be a step towards a new world polity that is better for Germany, because it diminishes German grievances by establishing more rights for the activities of German citizens. The peoples of the democratic allies refuse to countenance consideration of the generous tone of this new order. They resist appeals to understand its implications, and discuss friendliness with Germany only in proportion to Herr Hitler's threat of war.

17. Herr Hitler is misrepresented hypocritically and thoughtlessly. One facet of his nature is stressed to the heedless exclusion of all other sides. Ideal solutions for his problems are suggested wantonly. Difficulties that he must overcome, or which will overcome him, are ignored.

His leadership is caricatured as villainous and deranged. One who is a madman or a rogue is not accepted as leader of a modern civilised people. The unprecedented conditions in which he governs are unlike the orderliness and prosperity of the democratic powers. They are evolved from fearful apprehension of the disorderliness and poverty that might come about Germany as an outcome, among a divided people, of the indecisions of democratic methods. A modern dictator gains power by his outstanding ability in attempting difficult and disinterested ends. He survives tests of anxious friends, and ordeals of relentless enemies.

His supporters recognise in him a product of unique circumstances that require and perhaps create his particular services. His honour is in proportion to services demanded from extraordinary qualities in unexpected conditions. The willing submission, awful respect, and intense devotion inspired in his followers are in like proportion. The exigencies of Germany in contention with the democratic allies fall outside the willing comprehension of citizens of the democratic empires. Heedlessly they keep themselves unaware that their misconduct towards Germany has demonstrated again and again that the allied citizens, secure in their possessions, are obstinate enough never to consider German grievances, except at threat of war. Allied citizens decline to criticise themselves as others see them and refuse to look upon themselves from an honest German standpoint. The democratic citizens obstruct noble German desires for honest expansion. They refuse them as claims to rights. Unthinking, disregarding ignorance by allied citizens of honest German anxiety to establish new rights in a better world is an honourable cause of Herr Hitler's menacing attitude.

18. As it may be wrong to stress the brutality of Herr Hitler without understanding of its causes, so it may be wrong to stress the brutalities of exaggerated German nationalism to exclusion of sympathy with them. Fanatical hatred need never be taken seriously except when victim of its hypnotism are in unrestrained lawless conflict with the forces to which they attach their symbols of hatred. It is easy to torment and vilify Germans because Germans torment and vilify Jews. German nationalism is vainglorious and compensatory. Germans wish to gain benefit from their allied enemies, it would be untactful for them to vilify the allies. They cannot persecute them. Hatred is present. Resentment is instigated, as outlets for revenge are thwarted. The democratic peoples forget the extent to which Germans restrain from fanatical hatred against them. The symbols of German hatred either stupidly or rightly, are kept concentrated by German leadership, upon European Jewry and Communism. Emphatic German racialism is upright puritan refusal to countenance organised national self-blame. It is gallant evasion of wrong-headed shame, twisted acknowledgement of the retarded evolution of the German Empire, a demand that citizens of Germany be not compelled always to pay the penalty of unlucky delay. Thus it is a trumpet call to Germany, and an alarum for the rest of Europe. The monstrosities of pent-up German hatred are deflected from concentration upon German allied enemies by excessive racialism with its hideous accompaniment of deliberate and devilish persecution. The process is a mixture of calculated policy on the part of German leaders, with the awkward, self-conscious rhythm

of German repression. It is offensive but indirectly to the allies, an oblique expression of a sincere, and perhaps hopeless, desire for friendship.

19. "It seems to have been the considered policy of the British Government to govern its colonies by means of division", wrote Lord Durham, "and to break them down as much as possible into petty isolated communities, incapable of combination, and possessing no sufficient strength for individual resistance to the Empire." In a manner less conspicuous in regard to the harm to other peoples that is its outcome, this British policy seems to have been applied to the maintenance of a favourable balance of power in Europe.

The Germans need not be ashamed of their treatment of the allies, but the manners of allied citizens towards citizens of Germany are wanting in decency and consideration. German citizens are touchy, they are sensitive to rebuke, irony and misrepresentation. They dislike being treated as if unacceptable or undesirable. They examine and blame themselves for displaying resentment at ill-treatment from the allies. From the citizens and statesmen of the democratic empires they require, but do not possess, the force to demand that in a bargain or political arrangement, German enterprise and ambitions be valued upon the merits of honest German efforts. They are intolerant of depreciation of talented German endeavours. They resent that the democratic allies persist in trying to confine the activities of German citizens to music inside Germany, and outside Germany to buying and selling along with suspicious hostile citizens of the democratic empires. Such activities in relation to the world would not have satisfied Plato's ideal of a good citizen. The German ideal of a good citizen is not more likely to be satisfied. Germans have yet to learn how to confront individual allied slights as if they were the deliberate concerted insolence of the allied peoples. But advantages accruing from central control in totalitarian states teach them rapidly new means by which organisation may enforce vengeance by concentrating upon the inept vulnerabilities of democratic organisation. Collisions which made inevitable German intervention in the war concerning the murder at Sarajevo were not confined to quarrels concerning material objectives. Citizens of Germany labour under constant spiritual duress brought about by inability of allied citizens to resist taunting Germans with disguised incivility and injustice when Germans are unsupported in bargains, competitions or negotiations. The war of 1914-1918 defeated Germany and prevented realisation of the prospect of Hohenzollern conquest of Europe and the high seas. But defeat of Germany did not end the urgent but incoherent desires of the German peoples to establish rights to richer worldly activities in a spirit untarnished by heedless allied aspersions of ignobility. "No large community of free and intelligent men", wrote Lord Durham, "will long feel contented with a political system which places them, because it places their country, in a position of inferiority to their neighbours." It seems to the Germans that never will they be free from the perpetual trial of petty irritations. Thus, as a body the German race may be driven mad by torments, the incidence of which never can be described precisely. Relief for angry German feelings will be found either in just redress, or in violent outburst.

20. Implicit in the present problem is that the duty of clarifying issues falls upon allied statesmen. In

negotiations during a strike, settlement is not achieved by government subscribing to the attitude either of strikers, or of those resisting the strike. Terms of settlement depend upon interpretation by government of desires of all participants in the form of acceptable rights in relation to the polity of the state. The allied statesmen are both participators and mediators in the present European unrest. They are guardians of their own welfare and safety, and they are creators and guardians of the changing polity of the world. The allies, by authority established through their joint command of the seas and of many of the lands of the world claim to exercise privileges and duties of sovereign arbitrators. Implicit in the many duties of sovereignty is the obligation to strive to interpret the desires of all participants in disputes concerning rights, and to strive to arbitrate upon the meaning of sovereign interpretations. Thus the concern of allied statesmen is not confined to defense of their own interests, which are their responsibilities as participants. It is extended to guiding and controlling the general polity of all states in relation to the world.

In any conflict or collision in which there is appeal to sovereignty one set of forces is likely to be in combination in order to obtain power. Members combine in a trade union in order to obtain power to establish the rights of workers in relation to the polity of a state.

German citizens today combine in order to obtain power to establish the rights of Germans in relation to the polity of the world. In this dispute allied governments are embarrassed by being both sovereigns and participants. But a government is equally embarrassed in a great strike. Solutions for present causes of conflict are not likely to be such as are needed in order to prevent war, when embarrassed allied governments appeal to their supporters as participants in a quarrel. The British General Strike was not defeated by the peoples in the British Isles determining to repress the strikers. Conviction that government in the interest of the state would act fairly in relation both to the welfare of the state and the welfare of the strikers, defeated the inclination of the workers to maintain the British General Strike. Conviction that governments of the allies will act fairly in relation both to the welfare of the world and the welfare of German citizens will defeat the inclination of Germany to maintain warlike relations with the allies.

21. If the German offer of friendship is true, there is but one allied and British response to it. "True friendship can be found only among the virtuous", wrote Cicero. Friendship with Germany must include prospect of increasing benefit to citizens of the allied democracies and to citizens of Germany. It is beneficial to the allies to be free at once of the constant unnerving menace of airraids and of constant preparation against looming threats of war. To play for time and to affect to be lenient to Germany is to gamble with virtue and betray friendship. For citizens of the democratic empires to persuade themselves that it may be their duty to undertake so arduous and unprecedented an enquiry as should precede acceptance of German friendship is hard.

Before honourable friendship with Germany can be mooted old and new prejudices must be overcome. The re-introduction of Germany into imperial status, the incorporation of a changing Germany into the democratic allies, and the absorption of German citizens in the democratic empires are not regarded as practical policies.

There are similar impediments to successful allied and British negotiations with their own citizens than there are similar impediments for German statesmen. German statesmen now are entitled to speak for the right of Germany to expand, even if they are not certain how or where expansion shall take place. But sudden release by allied statesmen of unexpected proposals in relation to Germany, with far-reaching consequences throughout the wide world, would instigate conflicting and upsetting misapprehension. In all the domains of the democratic empires there would arise misunderstanding of claims of urgency and foresight. A friendship that is free from patronage and of value to Germany will demand sacrifice from the allies. Its proposal will be resented by the allied citizens who are called upon to bear the brunt of the sacrifices. Before 1914 the perspicacity and suspicion of citizens of the allied democracies excluded from honourable publicity embarrassed German claims for recognition of German rights to share in worldly enterprise. Today fair publicity to honest German desires for expansion appears equally shocking and fantastic. But public clarification of German ideas for alternatives to war is helpful and practical in the development of world polity, however shocking and fantastic German claims may seem to the more arrogant and intolerant of the allied citizens. Appeals for a new era of justice in the world should not be beyond the ability and imagination of allied statesmen now that the forces that surround the achievement of the world sovereignty demand that they shall be made. The Germans are eager for a new era, they will benefit from it. The allied citizens are complacent, being contented with the old order, they resist the new order because it will call upon them to make sacrifices. Until now none of the allied statesmen has been frank with the allied peoples as to how it has come about that the allied peoples are called upon to make sacrifices.

22. Let it be supposed that the German offer of friendship is not genuine and that the allied reciprocation of it is not serious. Negotiations are likely to be either long and demoralising, or to lead to immediate war. A time may come when airraids are no longer a menace, and when war in remote Europe is likely to be more destructive to Germany than to the allies. Allied negotiators will try to select a time when the allies can enter into a victorious war against a divided Germany, with least chance of their capital cities being destroyed. German negotiators will threaten the allied peoples to nervous exhaustion, and try to declare war in an atmosphere of panic. The effective alternative to demoralising negotiations and desultory war is a vigorous extirpation of the German Empire, and dispersal of the Germans. It seems that it is not contemplated. What seems to be contemplates is a *short* unprepared war now, or the exhaustion of Germany in the dredge and sludge of the mischampioned and defeated Austro-Hungarian Empire. Can immunity of London from air-raids be permitted to depend upon the caprice of Balkan politics? The immediate cause of the last European war lay in the incapacity of statesmen to control the diverse external forces riveted to the internal politics of the inflammable Balkan area. Another such war may be averted by deflecting the enterprise and energy of German citizens and the attentions of German high policy from absorption in protecting German peoples and their allies in lands infected for centuries by incalculable mischief. A world polity subjected to guidance or control from

motives that are best in relation to the progress of civilisation and human welfare is not likely to be established as an outcome of giving way to German demands for expansion in Eastern Europe by ill-considered stages in conflict with menace.

23. Statesmen who are responsible for the destinies of the allied peoples need bear no shame because they prepare to adjust their own colonial policy to the needs of the citizens of Germany. Accepting that the world is round, that there is but limited land to be colonised, and but few subject races who will suffer benefits of colonisation, presuming that colonisation is a combination of enterprising activities of good citizens in the interest of the progress of civilisation and of human welfare, and that attention should be paid to the claim of Germany that grievances of German citizens in regard to colonisation from a new category in world polity and justice, allowing that it is but a few years since earth and sea were explored, that the allied peoples are aware but imperfectly of the worldly sovereign power of allied statesmanship, and that vulnerability from the air and from ready military organisation of totalitarian states imperils world polity dependent upon sovereignty supported by naval hegemony and partial military domination of the land, allowing also that as participants in the present dispute concerning colonial rights the allied peoples are sluggish and complacent and that colonial policy is not commercial settlement, but preparation of subject races for fitting self-government, bearing in mind that these truths and likelihoods when remembered, in temperate reflection incontrovertible, and that they can be forgotten, as if valueless, during excitements of vital controversy and

preparation for war, the same, which are not inconsiderable in so far as the highest values are concerned, form a basis of friendly negotiation with Germany. By means of them war with Germany destructive to Europe may be avoided.

24. When passionate causes of war are vivid to peoples as to princes it is necessary to exchange hostages as pledges for mutual good faith. In the present dishonourable exigencies the same drastic type of international need arises. The reluctant allies are called upon to make sacrifices concerning their possessions. The enthusiastic Germans are called upon to refrain from violence. The allies cannot make world-wide concessions by a gesture. But they are vulnerable by a swift gesture from armed and eagerly alert Germans. That the allies now prefer negotiation to retaliation may not seem to Germans a pledge of honest goodwill, desire of the allies to evade war may seem to Germans like evidence of cunning deception. Friendly negotiations with Germany may be tested by the degree to which they make practicable ways and means related to ultimate German demands for rights to colonial expansion. If the basis of negotiations is frank and uncompromising, if it is formed with a view to arriving at an ultimate outcome which is favourable to German friendship, it will include recognition of German claims to colonial rights. An advertisement of this recognition will be a proper and bloodless victory for Germany. It will declare to the world the justice of the principles of a new category of claims. For Germany, this recognition of the German claim to colonial rights will be an invaluable and deathless hostage that throughout proceeding ages the allies will never be able to reclaim. If the recognition is used wisely by the Germans, the gain to justice achieved

in world polity will remain always to German credit. It will be an asset in the German demand that their just claim to rights to colonial activity be translated into practice.

25. The sacrifices demanded from the allied citizens are for the benefit of German citizens. In order to ease the difficulties of negotiation for the allies German statesmen must be prepared to accept on behalf of their citizens worldly loyalties that will ease negotiations by allowing the allies credit for exercising power and restraint in the interest of justice and world polity. In order to exercise their rights to colonial activity Germans either must try to seize allied sovereignty, or must contribute towards allied sovereignty by friendship. If the Germans decide to obviate failure to acquire worldly sovereignty for Germans by conquest, they will choose to exercise their rights to colonial activity by friendship with the allies. There will fall upon them, as upon the allies, duties of "conciliation and appeasement" that will be slow of complete accomplishment.

The choice of war or peace lies with the allies. The dominions of the allies are unwarlike. Except in defense of themselves and their motherlands, they will not resort to war. Along with the allies, they seek to make irresponsible war unlikely in the future. For, except by tarnishing the allies with dishonour, Czechoslovakia cannot retaliate upon them. Thus choice between ultimate victory for selfish satisfaction or magnanimous compromise for the sake of world polity, belongs to the allies. To allow the allies credit with their own peoples, and the peoples of the world for trying to solve without war by changes brought about through statesmanship quarrels that have hitherto led to war, rests with the Germans.

The most pressing immediate German interest is to satisfy almost ungovernable resentment of the humiliated German peoples. The most important ultimate German interest is to assure opportunities for German colonial enterprise. If in this case, as sometimes in an uncontrolled strike the immediate passionate interests of the rebels are satisfied to the point of savage indulgence, the effect upon world polity is likely to destroy confidence in the German right to claim privileges associated with the fulfillment of their ultimate interests in regard to colonisation. Rights to privilege never can be exercised without sovereign consent, except by an outlaw. Within any polity consent of the sovereign always must be won before interferences with privileges gained already receive sanction. Such consent is likely to be withheld from the Germans so long as Germany tries to intimidate German opponents. Primarily intimidation is a breach of friendship and sovereignty. If German citizens seek colonial expansion and only affect military domination as an instrument towards this end, German statesmen will comprehend that the allied decision to discuss interpretations of their rights is in the interest of justice and the polity of the world. Otherwise no concession can be granted to Germany, anywhere in the world, except as an outcome of a war provoked by Germany to arrest sovereignty from the allies. If this is the German mood, a destructive war blindly searching for European sovereignty is inevitable.

26. If, as the allied democracies and their dominions wish, war can be avoided by the forbearance of Germany during a period of honest negotiation, the allies cannot escape the grave responsibilities of recommending German colonial

expansion, wherever their sovereignty is obeyed, and German expansion is practical. Up to now the problems of German colonial expansion never have been considered with a will to making that expansion practicable in the interests of justice and world polity. The revolutionary change of mind implies a new approach to negotiations. Such a decision once taken, to suspect German intrusion no longer is desirable. The task of friendship is to enquire what benefits can be derived from accepting German help in colonial responsibility. Not only is it plausible, but also it is likely, that with the help of British persuasion some natural subject peoples may be led to accept German rule, on the ground that they may derive greater benefits from German rule than they now derive from exclusive British and allied rule. But world revolutionary changes could not take place upon a scale satisfying to calls upon the allies when accepting honourable friendship with Germany, without consent of the British Dominions, including the Union of South Africa. The Germans must be brought to comprehend that such consent will not be won by threats of air-raids upon London and Paris. It is likely to be won only upon the complex assurance that Europe is united in defending an ideal polity for the world, in providing the best colonial expansion for inferior races, and the best type of military protection for them. Only upon this complex basis of restrained appeal with peoples in many parts of the world be led to understand that the well-being of their inhabitants and the prosperity of their industries may benefit from resources of German personnel and capital. Only upon recognition by Germany of German intention to accept a joint duty with the allies towards the creation and exercise of world sovereignty, will the peoples of the democratic empires be persuaded not to decline benefits they might receive as an outcome of closer association with the citizens of Germany.

27. The era of national guardian states for subject races already is upon the wane. But except as an outcome of war or disorderliness there can be no swift change towards international control or control of subject races by joint guardian states, certainly not at the behest of restive Germans. Modern armaments being as they are, and the danger of widespread conflagration what it is, swift changes are uncontemplatible until disputes in regard to command of the sea and the land are placed in abeyance for the sake of civilisation and human welfare.

Yet the time approaches when precedence in colonial management will be exposed to the test of world sovereignty. Commerce has become increasingly international, in some parts of the world it possesses sovereign authority. Already government by a single guardian state is resented by the subject race least when advantages to the subject race may be stressed in terms of services rendered to the subject race, concealing the advantages the returns for these services bring to the guardian state. The standard of entrance by examination into all public services would be raised by the admission of Germans. Throughout the British Empire there are many services for subject races which would be better performed by Germans according to improved modern standards than by Englishmen now available. The progress of German citizens into the British Empire by examination and by way of relaxation of immigration laws in favour of German citizens is likely to be a slow affair. But it is agreed by the allied statesmen that Germany is to be trusted as a friend, the difficulties that arise must be overcome somehow by statesmanship.

The British Empire lags behind ideals which its best statesmen have set up for it. Its progress towards fitting self-government is not in proportion to the many claims for service the duties of imperial responsibility impose upon the motherland. Not every facet of the evolution of a great modern empire is covered by naval hegemony, the varied work of a highly trained governing class, and by commercial activities. The framework of empire is kept together by this indispensable structure. But it is no better for the polity of the world that empire should be kept together by the skeletons of its framework than that Europe should be plunged into wanton war. Unexpected calls today are being made upon the personnel of all empires. Throughout the British Empire subject races are deprived of the full benefits of many services that are rendered to them by the exclusive character of British and allied imperialism. Elementary, secondary and higher education, journalism and broadcasting, are now as cardinal in their relations to good imperial development as in the past have been honest administration and military protection. The provincial universities of the allied motherlands are not equal to the great demand for teachers, schoolmasters, broadcasters, journalists and expert professional men of all types, made by the allied empires. Syrians, Chinese, Cypriots and Maltese are permitted to undertake arduous and skilled work that could be performed better by Germans. These many vital services, inadequately performed are causes of unrest, and would be provided properly if the quality of man-power were available. In many parts of the allied empire service is called for that neither can be supplied nor paid for. German skill, enthusiasm, and wealth should not be declined wantonly on a mistaken theory of narrow imperialism.

The means of making German services acceptable should be explored in the interest of progress of civilisation and of general welfare. It is contrary to the best ideas of world sovereignty that enquiry into ways and means of German expansion should be discouraged in deference to suspicion.

28. The time has come when war between civilised states must be looked upon as rebellion against world order, as a practical policy in the interests of civilisation and human welfare. The bloodshed and devastation of rebellion are undesirable. The permanent triumph of selfish and oppressive men by outlawing rights to rebellion equally is undesirable. There is always likelihood that the rebellious are right, at least concerning the justice of their grievances, and that the forces which resist rebellion resist, because of the unwillingness of good citizens to adapt themselves to experiments in untried conditions. The interest of state polity lies in trying to co-ordinate the indignation that promotes change with the cautious hesitancy which seeks to conserve good as it is. The role of the British Empire in the rapidly changing circumstances of the world is not made easier by belittling its relations to the changing tone of world polity, or by exaggerating its importance to itself. Scarcely it is likely that the British Empire can exist side by side with the enmity and resentment of German peoples without war. Not from the standpoint of the world, nor of Britain, nor of the allies, nor of Germany, is the brewing vortex of Europe likely to be suffocated or controlled by the self-

emphasis of one patriotism or another. Patriotic feelings need to be inspired and directed towards common ends of good world government. If general conviction can be established that the grievances of Germany are being regarded by the allied governments with charity and resolute determination to test them and remedy them, they are not more unusual, disturbing, and menacing in relation to the establishment of world polity than the grievances of a trade union, or of the Trade Union Congress in relation to the polity of the British Empire.

# SADLERIANA-BIBLIOGRAPHY

A glance at Sadler's abundant publications below, their depth and breadth, not to mention the beauty and lucidity of the language, make him a most remarkable, modern educational thinker, scholar and philosopher.
The following three works are particularly useful:

PICKERING, O.S.. *Sir Michael Sadler, A Chronological Bibliography.* Some 600 items are listed and the source where many of them may be found is indicated. This publication is available from the Department of Adult and Continuing Education, University of Leeds, Leeds LS2 9JT, United Kingdom. (Stuart Marriott's "Biographical Introduction" to Sadler is well worth reading carefully.)

HIGGINSON, J.H. (ed.). *Selections from Michael Sadler.* Liverpool, Dejall & Meyorre, 1980. (ISBN 090560301-X.) This book is now out of print, but copies exist in many university libraries across the world. These "Selections" enable Sadler to speak for himself directly to the reader who will be his own interpreter.

HIGGINSON, J.H.. A UNESCO-Publication, 'Profiles of Educators' – Michael Ernest Sadler (1861-1943), *Prospects*, Vol. XX, No. 4, 1990.

**For general biographies, consult:**

SADLEIR, Michael. *Michael Ernest Sadler: Memoir by his Son.* London, Constable, 1949.
GRIER, Lynda. *Achievements in Education: The Work of Michael Ernest Sadler (1885-1935).* London, Constable, 1952.

**Monumental publications by M. E. Sadler:**

| | |
|---|---|
| 1893 | *University Extension, Past, Present and Future*, by M.E. Sadler and J.H. Mackinder. London, Cassell. |
| 1897-1902 | *Special Reports on Educational Subjects.* Issued by the Office of Special Inquiries and Reports under the direction of M.E. Sadler, these volumes contain informed papers by Michael Sadler and also illustrate his talent for finding colleagues with particular knowledge of other systems of education.<br>Vol. 1 (1897). Education in England, Wales, Ireland, France, Germany, Denmark, Belgium.<br>Vol. II (1898). Education in England and Wales; Physical Education; The Heuristic Method of Teaching; University Education in France.<br>Vol. III (1898). National Organisation of Education in Switzerland; Secondary Education in Prussia, Baden and Sweden; Teaching of Modern Languages; Higher Commercial Education in France, Germany and Belgium.<br>Vol. IV (1901). Educational Systems of the Dominium of Canada, Newfoundland and the West Indies. |

| | |
|---|---|
| 1936 | 'The Scholarship System in England to 1890'. Published in *Essays on Examinations*, for the International Institute Examinations Inquiry. In this volume, which he edited, Sadler also included 'The Leaving Examination as Conducted in the Secondary Schools of Prussia', reprinted from the *Report* of the Royal Commission on Secondary Education in 1895. |
| 1941 | 'Juncta Disjuncta'. These five articles, reprinted in *The Times* of London as an eight-page pamphlet, cover the following themes: 'The English Public Schools'; 'Future of the Private Schools'; 'The Troubled Sea of the Mind'; 'The Two-mindedness of England about Education'; and 'A Ministry of Health and Education'. (The fourth article is reprinted in Higginson, *op. cit.*, "Selections", pp. 187-9.) |

The writer is also aware of the existence of many papers and MSS by M.E. Sadler not listed above.

he was President. Calcutta, Superintendent of Government Printing.

1926 *Our Public Elementary Schools.* London, Thornton Butterworth.

Introduction to *The Folk High Schools of Denmark* (by Holger Begtrup, Hans Lund, Peter Manniche), pp. 5-8. London, Oxford University Press.

1928 *Thomas Day: An English Disciple of Rousseau.* (The Rede Lecture.) Cambridge, Cambridge University Press.

1930 'The Outlook in Secondary Education'. Three lectures published in *The Teachers College Record* (New York, Columbia University).

'The Philosophy Underlying the System of Education in England', Part 1. In: I.L. Kandel (ed.), *Education Yearbook of the International Institute of the Teachers College, Columbia University.*

1934 Introduction to Tagore at Shantinekatan, or A Survey of Dr. Rabindranath Tagore's Educational Experiments at Shantinekatan. Bombay, H. Chaturdevi.

1935 'Bibliography Relating to Indigenous Art in Tropical Africa' and 'Significance and Vitality in African Art' – two articles contributed by Sadler to Arts of West Africa (which he edited). London, Oxford University Press for the International Institute of African Languages and Cultures.

*John Adams. A Lecture in his Memory.* Published by the Oxford University Press for the London Institute of Education.

Vol. V (1901). Educational Systems of Cape Colony, Natal, Commonwealth of Australia, New Zealand, Ceylon and Malta.
Vol. VI (1900). Preparatory Schools for Boys: Their Place in British Secondary Education.
Vol. VII (1902). Rural Education in France.
Vol. VIII (1902). Education in Scandinavia, Switzerland, Holland, Hungary.
Vol. IX (1902). Education in Germany.
Vol. X (1902). Education in the U.S.A. Part 1.
Vol. XI (1902). Education in the U.S.A. Part 2.

**Key publications by M. E. Sadler:**

| | |
|---|---|
| 1903-23 | *'Education in England'*. (Monthly letters to the review *Indian Education*). London, Longman, Green & Co.. |
| 1903-06 | *Reports* specially commissioned by local education authorities seeking to reorganise their education provision after the 1902 Education Act. |
| 1907 | *Continuation Schools in England and Elsewhere.* Manchester University Press. |
| 1908 | *Moral Instruction and Training in Schools.* (Report of an international inquiry.) London, Longman, Green & Co.. |
| 1911 | *Report on Education in Guernsey.* |
| 1919 | *Report of the Commission on the University of Calcutta.* 5 vols.. Edited by Michael Sadler along with other members of the Commission of which |

# INDEX

## A

Abyssinia, 28
Adolf Hitler, 13, 29, 39
Adult Education, 2
Africa, 2, 45, 73, 82
allies, 45, 50, 52, 56, 57, 58, 60, 61, 62, 63, 65, 66, 67, 68, 70, 71, 73, 77
American colleges, 2
Anglo-German Review, 15, 24
anti-Semitism, 30
Aristotelian constitution, 4
Asia, 2, 45
Austria, 52
Austro-Hungarian Empire, 68

## B

BBC, 33, 40
Bolshevism, 11
Boys of the City, 28
British Empire, 39, 43, 53, 56, 74, 75, 76
British General Strike, 66
Bryce Commission on Secondary Education, 4

## C

Canada, 12
casus belli, 27
censorship, 17
Chamberlain, 31
China, 34
Christ Church College, 35
Cicero, 66
citizens, 44, 45, 47, 48, 49, 50, 51, 52, 54, 55, 57, 58, 59, 60, 61, 62, 63, 66, 67, 69, 71, 72, 74, 75, 76
class, 29, 46, 48, 75
class distinctions, 29
colonial expansion, 45, 70, 72, 73
colonies, 38, 43, 44, 45, 48, 50, 52, 54, 63
colonisation, 47, 51, 56, 69, 72
Columbia University, 3
Comparative Education, xi
Comparative Educationist, x
competition, 46
concentration camps, 29
Contemporary Review, 3
Crusade of Propaganda, 31
cultural life, 29
Czechoslovakia, 30, 31, 43, 60, 72

## D

democracies, 50, 52, 66, 67, 73
Denmark, 10
diary, 28, 29, 30, 31, 33
Director of the Office of Special Inquiries and Reports, 2, 9
Dr. James Harry Higginson, 36

## E

Eastern Europe, 45, 57, 69
Economic Revolution, 34
economics, 27, 37
educated classes, 15
Educational Intelligence, 42
educational institutions, x
educational organisation, 5, 7
educational research, 5
educational systems, x, 18
English Civil War, 4
Englishness, 3
Europe, 1, 2, 13, 16, 20, 30, 34, 43, 45, 47, 52, 53, 55, 56, 57, 58, 59, 60, 63, 64, 68, 70, 73, 75, 77
European Common Market, 34
experimental teaching, 9

## F

Factory Acts, 1
Fascism, 19
*Faust*, 1
First World War, 27, 37, 38
Foreign Office, 33, 35
France, 6, 7, 13, 30, 45, 53, 55, 80, 81
Franco-Russian Pact, 28
freedom, 14, 15, 16, 19, 29, 52, 59

## G

general polity, 49, 54, 65

George Washington's Farewell Address, 2
German citizens, 49, 51, 52, 53, 57, 59, 60, 63, 66, 69, 71, 75
German Empire, 39, 62, 68
German nationalism, 62
German people, 30, 33
Germany, 3, 6, 7, 9, 11, 12, 13, 15, 16, 17, 18, 19, 20, 22, 24, 27, 28, 29, 33, 34, 37, 38, 39, 40, 41, 45, 52, 53, 55, 57, 58, 59, 60, 61, 62, 63, 66, 67, 68, 69, 70, 72, 73, 75, 77, 80, 81
governmental control, 5

## H

Herr Joachim von Ribbentrop, 39
Herr von Ribbentrop, 11
higher education, 6, 75
Hitler, 10, 11, 12, 15, 17, 18, 20, 21, 30, 31, 59, 60, 61, 62
Hobbes, 49, 50
home training, 7
human welfare, 69, 74, 76

## I

imperialism, 34, 75
Intelligence Activities, 42
international colonial problem, 43, 44
Italy, 19, 21, 22, 28, 45, 53

## J

James Seth Memorial Lecture, 16
Japan, 13, 34, 45
Jews, 59, 62
John Ruskin, x
John Stuart Mill, x, 21
journalism, 75
journalists, 36, 75

## L

League of Nations, 43
Leeds University, 4, 6
liberal education, 20, 21
Lord Durham, 63, 64
Lord Halifax, 33

## M

Maginot Line, 55
Manifesto on Peace and Cooperation, 31, 40
Matthew Arnold, xi
media, 3
Mein Kampf, 13, 18, 19
Mellin Nahrung, 10
melting pot, xii, 2, 6
Memorandum, 35, 36, 40, 41, 42
middle classes, 46
militarism, 21
military oppression, 58
Monroe Doctrine, 45
moral reconditioning, 14
MSS, 35, 36, 38, 41, 83
Mussolini, 21, 31, 34

## N

national education, 5, 18
national educational system, x
National Socialism, 10, 11
nationalism, 20, 34
Nazi Revolution, 14, 15
Nazism, 19

## O

Office of Special Inquiries and Reports, 41, 80
Oxford, v, 1, 2, 4, 11, 21
Oxford University, 1

## P

patriotism, 77
Plato, 64
Poland, 28
politics, 37, 39, 68
popular education, 5
poverty, 46, 61
press, 17
Professor Jack Sislian, xi
propaganda, 13, 16, 28, 30, 58, 60
Prussia, 38, 57, 80, 83
public service, 19, 20

## Q

Queen Elisabeth, 55, 56

## R

race, 43, 65, 74
racialism, 62
repression, 29, 63
revolution, 22
Rhine, 34, 56
rights, 47, 48, 49, 50, 51, 52, 58, 60, 62, 64, 65, 66, 67, 70, 71, 72, 76
Roman Empire, 59
romanticism, xii
Russia, 13, 19, 22, 28

## S

scholarship, 1, 5, 7, 36
Scotland, 55, 56
Second World War, 27, 33, 36, 38
self-control, 20
self-expression, 48
social ideals, 8
social reform, 57
social relationships, 8, 13
social systems, 38
self-training, 7

Shakespeare, 21
South America, 45
sovereign authority, 43, 74
Soviet Communism, 19
sovereignty, 44, 53, 58, 59, 65, 68, 69, 71, 72, 73, 74, 76
statesmanship, 48, 69, 72, 75
statesmen, 44, 47, 48, 51, 55, 56, 57, 58, 59, 60, 63, 65, 67, 69, 71, 72, 75
State control of education, 3
Sudeten, 52, 60
Sudetendeutschland, 31, 34

## T

Third Reich, 19, 22, 36, 39
totalitarian states, 17, 53, 64, 69
trade, i, 3
Trade Union Congress, 77
two-mindedness, 30

## U

University of Manchester, 4

## V

Versailles Treaty, 13
violence, 29, 30, 70

## W

war, 27, 28, 30, 31, 32, 33, 34, 38, 39, 41, 43, 47, 48, 51, 52, 53, 54, 55, 57, 60, 62, 64, 66, 67, 68, 70, 71, 72, 73, 74, 75, 76
War Aims, 34
Weimar Republic, 10, 11
Weltanschauung, 38
Whitcliffe Mount School, 6
World Education, 3
world polity, 37, 56, 58, 59, 60, 67, 69, 71, 72, 73, 76